THE McGRAW-HILL HANDBOOK OF MORE BUSINESS LETTERS

THE McGRAW-HILL HANDBOOK OF MORE BUSINESS LETTERS

ANN POE

McGraw-Hill

New York   San Francisco   Washington, D.C.   Auckland
Bogotá   Caracas   Lisbon   London   Madrid   Mexico City
Milan   Montreal   New Delhi   San Juan   Singapore
Sydney   Tokyo   Toronto

Library of Congress Cataloging-in-Publication Data

Poe, Ann
    The McGraw-Hill handbook of more business letters / Ann Poe.
      p.   cm.
    Includes index.
    ISBN 0-07-050517-9 (alk. paper)
    1. Commercial correspondence—Handbooks, manuals, etc. I. Title.
  HF5726.P545   1998
  651.7'5—dc21   98-24855
                                                     CIP

McGraw-Hill

*A Division of The **McGraw·Hill** Companies*

4 5 6 7 8 9 0 DOC/DOC 0 3

ISBN 0-07-050517-9

The sponsoring editor for this book was Betsy Brown, the editing supervisor was Fred Dahl, and the production supervisor was Pamela Pelton. It was typeset in Palatino by Inkwell Publishing Services.

Printed and bound by R. R. Donnelley & Sons, Inc.

To

Roy W. Poe

When we see a natural style, we are quite surprised and delighted, for we expected to see an author and we find a man.

Blaise Pascal, *Pensées*

Contents

About This Book

Part I contains more than 50 tips and suggestions to help you make the most of today's business communication technology. You'll learn what business correspondence is all about and how to make your letters, memos, and faxes look great. This section offers ideas on how to enhance your message to make it as effective as possible.

Part II contains over 300 sample letters, representing a variety of business situations. These letters can be adapted and used to suit your needs.

Each sample letter is a simple outline, a skeleton letter. Each offers a way to start and a way to end. It suggests a focus, a direction to help make your writing clearer. These letters are intentionally nonspecific so they will be easier to adapt to your particular situation.

Pick a letter that seems as though it might work. Start inserting relevant details—names, circumstances, dates for follow-up. Depending on the situation, you might want to summarize events, make a recommendation, ask for additional information, summarize what needs to be done, or say thank you. Modify the model letter—add, delete, make changes until it works.

The final letter is likely to be longer than the original model, but now it is your own. The letter documents your business. It conveys your information, and it has taken on your voice and your style. It is a bridge between you and your reader.

Acknowledgments

Many friends and associates offered advice and encouragement, and this book is better because of their input. I especially want to thank the following people:

Glenn Benham, Robert Blazier, Betsy Brown, Deborah Churan, Linda Cunningham, Bruce Ferguson, Howard Fiedler, Vicky Fleites, Mary Jane Gill, Philip Haley, Marian Hardin, Daniel Haughey, Kris Jackson, Edward Maestro, Norma Maestro, Alan Merkle, Lynn Mills, Sonny Nardulli, Michael O'Connor, James O'Malley, Martin Parrish, Joseph Pezdirtz, Christopher Poe, David Poe, Elizabeth Poe, Silvia Realzola, Fran Russo, Michael Sarkady, Kandy Schneider, Roy Voigt, John Winings, Thomas Winings.

THE ———— McGRAW-HILL HANDBOOK OF MORE BUSINESS LETTERS

Part I

Introduction

The letters we write are a reflection of ourselves, who we are and how we conduct our business. Our letters help us get customers, keep customers, communicate with employees, and show our associates that they are appreciated. We want our letters to be professional without being cold, comfortable and familiar without being cute. We want a response—perhaps a sale to a new customer, or payment on an overdue invoice from another customer. Or we want to maintain a good business relationship by thanking one person for a tip or congratulating another on a promotion.

Business letters have changed. They tend to be shorter and more to the point, and we write more of them. We no longer have time to impress the addressee with our stylish and perfectly crafted letter. We are pressured to write quickly so we can deal with the next situation, and the next, and the next.

The ways we write have changed, too. Other than adding our signature to a document or filling out a form, we rarely write in longhand anymore. Instead we "process words" on a computer. We no longer have assistants to take our dictation and correct our spelling and grammar mistakes—we have to do it ourselves. We use our computers to compose, edit, and print our letters, then send them via electronic mails—fax, e-mail, and voice mail.

These are still written communications (even voice mail is best approached that way), and the principles of good letter writing apply. Communication technology changes, but the need to send an effective message and maintain good relationships with our customers and associates remains the same.

Using Your Computer Effectively

Computers have caused fundamental changes in the way we communicate and do business. Business letters are delivered on paper via regular or express mail, on a computer screen as an e-mail message, on tape as a recorded voice message, or digitized and transmitted via fax machine. The latest generation of beepers display brief written messages as well as phone numbers and soon will transmit voice messages as well. The ability to use your personal computer for tele-conferencing and video mail is just around the corner.

Get the Most from Your Computer

Although most businesspeople have computers, few users take full advantage of this powerful tool. Turning yourself into a "power user" may seem daunting, but computers are easier to master than you might think. Every hour you spend learning what your system can do will save you untold hours in the future. It's time to overcome your fears and dive into those help files. Here are some sure-fire ways to improve your computer skills.

Practice.

The more you use your system, the easier it gets. A power user is simply an experienced user.

Fiddle with your system and overcome your fears. Discover several ways to do any given task. Get comfortable using keyboard commands, function keys, and tables. Experiment with different features, looking for those that will be most useful in your business.

Get a tutor.

Ask at your computer store about personal tutors. It might be worth the fee to have a few private lessons, one on one.

You can also enlist a coworker or patient friend who is already comfortable with the system. Most people like to show off their skills and are willing to teach others. Be sure, though, that you're the one sitting in front of the terminal, not your friend. Your friend already knows how to make it work.

Take a course.

Community colleges and computer stores offer a variety of classes for new users and experienced programmers alike. Try an introductory course, or take a class on the software program you use most often at work. If you use the hunt-and-peck method on the keys, take a keyboarding class first. You can also buy a course. Look for specialized audio and video tapes.

Read the manual; buy a book.

Thumb through the manuals that accompany software programs and hardware components. You may not understand everything, but at least you'll know what's covered and where to look the next time you're stuck.

Then head for your bookstore. There are many excellent books that match your level of expertise and interest, whether it's using a particular software program or programming in a certain language.

Ask your children.

They have been playing computer entertainment games and learning basic computer skills since kindergarten or even earlier. Where you're fearful, your kids are not. What is foggy to you will be obvious to them. Let them show you the ropes. They'll be delighted to be smarter than you for once.

Make your home system compatible with your office system.

Install the same software on your home computer so that you can transport files on a disk. Set up the same in-files and out-files on both systems so you can quickly copy the most recent update from one to the other.

Take advantage of the latest modem technology.

A modem is the phone connection between your computer and the rest of the world. Use your modem to connect to the Internet or another computer. You'll appreciate the convenience of checking office e-mail from home or while traveling. If you're on a trip and left an important presentation file at home or at the office, it will be essential that you be able to connect to that computer and download what you need. Most modems allow your computer to send and receive faxes, too.

Master everything in a software package.

Professional business software packages typically include word processing, database, spreadsheet programs, and more. The advantage is that information in one program can be imported easily to another. With just a few keystrokes, a table from your spreadsheet program can be copied into the report you're writing with your word processing software. Commands like cut and paste are the same, so if you are proficient in one program, your skills will transfer to the next one.

Integrated programs are excellent if your job includes a variety of tasks, both big and small. Too many people use only one program, ignoring the rest. They may be unaware that they can schedule appointments, send and receive faxes, maintain a client database, run statistical analyses, remind themselves when something is due, create a slide presentation and project it from a laptop, use an address book to print out a letter and envelope together, and on and on.

Make your own database of letter parts.

If you routinely write letters on the same subject, store key paragraphs separately, then insert them into new letters as needed. This system works best if you are writing to different people all the time. It's not a good idea to send the same person or business a string of letters that are identical.

Your database should also include names, addresses, and phone numbers of your business contacts. Learn how to use mail merge so you can send one letter to many recipients.

Respect the limits of your software.

Programs that check spelling and grammar are helpful, but not foolproof. Usage errors will still slip through. Use these programs, but proofread your work anyway. If your language skills are poor, go back to school. A mastery of English will always be a requirement for business success.

Back up your work.

The reality is that like all machines, computers sometimes fail. Always keep backup files of your work by copying data onto a disk regularly. Consider installing a special backup drive on your system. If a project is hot, back up files at least once a day. Name your files as soon as you open them, and save, save, save.

Be aware of security issues.

Remember that files are easily lost to the novice, but to the computer hacker, nothing is ever completely lost. Most systems make copies of everything on the computer for system use; this means that a delete is not always a complete delete. In most cases, a delete means the file is available to be overwritten, but the information has not necessarily disappeared. A skilled hacker can access files or file fragments long after you are certain they have disappeared from existence.

Discover the Internet

In recent years, more and more businesses have started using the Internet. The Net is indeed an information superhighway and global network. You can receive stock quotations and other financial data, check weather around the globe, stay informed about today's business news, get information about other companies, locate people, look at maps, plan trips, research special interests, and more.

If your business is not already wired into the Internet, it's easy to connect. An Internet provider will give you browsing software and instructions on what hardware you'll need to complete your connection. Charges vary, but generally you can expect to pay a monthly or hourly fee to your provider, plus the cost of the connection.

To find information, your Web browsing software will help you connect to an on-line search engine. Simply enter a key word or phrase and the search begins. Each search engine will give you instructions on sophisticated ways to narrow the search.

Be aware, however, that not all the information you find is valid. There are no limits as to who makes announcements or what is posted, and much of the information available does not come from legitimate sources. Before you use any information found on the Net, make sure you know who is sponsoring a particular Web site and why.

Businesses with Web sites provide information and easy access to their customers. If you want to set up a Web site, the most prudent course of action would be to hire an expert who can design an effective site and make it accessible to your customers. If you are unsure what to put on your Web site, the best place for ideas is the Net itself. Surf around, visit competitors' Web sites, and take a look at the information presented by other companies.

Business Resources When Traveling

Business travel used to mean that certain tasks had to be postponed until you returned to the office. Now you can take your office with you.

Travel with a laptop computer and a portable printer. These are small, lightweight, and just as powerful as the big ones back at the office. Add a fax/modem and you can turn any phone line into an on-line connection. If you connect to the Internet while traveling, find out if your Internet service provider has a toll-free access number.

When you're in your hotel room, you can generate correspondence, print it out, or send it from your computer as fax or e-mail messages. While you're on-line, check stock prices and get the local weather forecast. Airports and hotels that cater to the business traveler offer fax, photocopier, and other related services. Some even have computers available in case you left yours at home.

If you have to deliver a presentation or report while you're on the road, pick up a phone book to see if there is a 24-hour computer and copy service available. These businesses offer computers, faxes, photocopying, binding, Internet access, and all the office supplies you might need. A few notes scratched on the back of a napkin at the airport can be turned into several bound sets of full-color reports by morning.

Remember that local public libraries can be helpful, too. Many offer business services as well as research materials—and often at very little cost. The reference room of the public library may have just what you need for that on-the-road project.

Figure 1.

① **Company Name**
   Street Address
   City, State Zip
   Phone, Fax

② Today's date

③ Recipient's Name
   Title
   Company Name
   Address
   City, State Zip

④ Re: [optional]

⑤ Dear Name:

⑥ Body of letter, paragraph 1 xxx x xx xx xxx xx xxxx xxxx xxx xx xxxx xxx xxx
   xxxxx xxx xx xx xxx xx xx x xxxxxxxx xxx xx xx xxxx xxxx xxx xx xxxx xxx xxx
   xxxxx xxx xx xx xxx xx xx x xxxxxx xxx x xxx xxx xx xxxx xxx xx xxxx.

   Body of letter, paragraph 2 xxx x xx xx xxx xx xxxx xxxx xxx xx xxxx xxx xxx
   xxxx xxxx xx xxx xxx xx xx x xxx xxxx xxx xx xx xxxx xxxx xxx xx xxxx xxx xxx
   xxxxx xxx xx xx xxx xx xx x xxxxx xx xxxx xxx xxx xxxx xxx xx xx xxx xx.

   Body of letter, paragraph 3 xxx x xx xx xxx xx xxxx xxxx xxx xx xxxx xxx xxx
   xxxxx xxx xxxx xxx xx xx x xx xxxxxx xxx xx xx xxxx xxxx xxx xx xxxx.

⑦ Closing,

⑧ *Signature*

   Sender's Name
   Title

⑨ cc: Name
      Name

⑩ encl.

⑪ ABC/def

Letters

Business letters are set up in a standard format, one that has been around for years. There are many variations, but the one shown in Figure 1 is perhaps the most popular. It is easy to set up and always looks professional.

Here are the elements of a business letter:

1. Letterhead

The letterhead is at the top of the page. It includes the company name, address, and phone number. Fax numbers and e-mail addresses can be included, too. The letterhead design can be printed on blank stationery or scanned onto a hard disk. To design your own letterhead, use a template that comes with your word processor or simply center the information at the top of the page.

2. Today's date

This is the date the letter is mailed, not the day you started writing it. Position it flush left or flush right, or tab to the center of the page and start typing.

Position the date three to five lines down from the last line of the letterhead. If you're using preprinted stationery, try starting on the seventh line down from the top of the page to avoid overprinting.

3. Addressee information

This includes name, title, company name, and address. Note that each item is flush left on a new line. If you are unsure about any information, pick up the phone and call the business. The person who answers either will know or can find out.

Use Mr., Mrs., Miss, or Ms. with the person's name. If the title is short, it can appear on the same line as the name. If it is long, it should be on a separate line. For example:

Ms. Sally Smith, Manager

Or:

Ms. Sally Smith
Manager, Retail Sales

Type company name and address as it appears on letterhead. Do not abbreviate words like *Street, Road,* or *Avenue.* Spell out states or use the two-letter Post Office abbreviations. Note that there is a space, but no comma, between the state and zip code.

Position the first line (addressee name) five lines down from the date.

4. Attention line (optional)

This is a reference line. It starts with either *Attention* or *Re* and is followed by a colon. It can refer to a person, a specific item, or the subject of the letter. For example:

Attention: Accounts Receivable
Attn: John Doe
Re: Purchase Order A-1234 dated August 3, 19xx
Re: XYZ Project

Position the attention line two lines down from the addressee's city/state/zip line.

5. Salutation

This reads Dear Whoever and ends with a colon. Position it flush left and two lines down from the attention line or the addressee's city/state/zip line. If you know the person, you can use the first name. If not, use Mr., Mrs., Miss, or Ms. and the last name. If you have no idea who will be handling your letter, use Dear Sir or Madam. For example:

Dear John:
Dear Mr. Doe:
Dear Sir or Madam:

6. Body of letter

The typical business letter has three paragraphs. You can choose to indent or not. A paragraph can be one sentence long. In fact, the entire letter can consist of one sentence. Yes, this would make your high school English teacher nuts, but you're writing a business letter, not a term paper.

The first paragraph starts two lines down from the salutation.

7. Closing

The closing is followed by a comma. Position the closing flush left or tab to the center of the page and start typing. Common closings used today are:

Sincerely,	Warm regards,
Sincerely yours,	Best wishes,
Regards,	Cordially,
Best regards,	Yours truly,

8. *Name, title, and signature*

Type your full name (first name, middle initial, and last name) three or four lines down from the closing. Your title goes on the next line. Both are lined up flush left with the closing. Your signature goes in the space above your typed name.

9. *Copies*

List other people who are getting a copy of the letter. Use *cc* followed by a colon. For example:

cc: John Doe
   Mary Smith

The abbreviation *cc* stands for *carbon copy; Xc (Xerox copy)* is also used. If someone is getting a secret copy, use *bcc* (blind carbon copy). This notation appears on the blind and file copies only. Blind copies have their place, but should never be used to be inappropriately secretive or bypass a supervisor.

cc: John Doe
   Mary Smith
bcc: Sam Jones

The *cc*, or distribution, list is positioned flush left and two or more lines down from your title.

10. *Enclosures*

If extra material is enclosed with the letter, note this with *Encl.* or *Enclosure*. If desired, you can state the number of attachments. For example:

Enclosure
Enclosures (3)
Encl. (2)

Enclosure notation is positioned flush left and two or more lines down from the distribution list. How many lines of space you drop down depends on how much room you have left at the bottom of the page.

11. *Initials*

If the letter is written or dictated by one person and typed by another, this is noted using each person's initials. The first set of initials is in upper case and refers to the writer. The second set is in lower case and refers to the assistant. Initials are separated by a slash.

For example, if Mary D. Smith dictates a letter to Sally P. Jones, the notation is:

MDS/spj

If there are no initials, the reader can assume you are the writer.

Initials are positioned flush left under copies and enclosures. You can double-space or not, depending on the length of the letter.

Make Your Letters Look Good

Visual presentation counts. An attractive letter makes a good impression—the paper feels good; the letter is pleasing to the eye. The reader assumes that the writer is competent and professional, even before reading the first word.

Like it or not, how your letter looks is part of your message. To make your letters look great, consider these basics:

Center the letter on the page.

The letter should be centered top and bottom, right and left. Start with 1-inch margins at the top and bottom of the page. Use 1¼-inch margins on each side. You can change them as needed, but these margins will work for most letters.

Make every line flush left.

Each line should be aligned at the same place on the left-hand side. The right-hand margin can be uneven. The word processing program will wrap each line automatically.

Use single spacing. Double-space between paragraphs.

The extra line of space between paragraphs gives the reader's eye a place to rest. A paragraph indent (indenting the first word of each paragraph five spaces) is optional if there is double spacing between paragraphs.

Aim for three paragraphs.

This rule is made to be broken, but it's a good place to start. Using three paragraphs adds balance to the overall look of the page, even if one of those paragraphs is only one sentence long.

Use one subject per letter.

Limit each letter to one subject. If you have two items to discuss, write two separate letters.

The letter should fit on one page.

There are many letters longer than one page, but the point is valid. If your letter is dribbling over onto a second sheet, reread it. See if you can delete some extra lines of space, adjust the margins slightly, rework a few sentences, and make it fit onto one page. Take care that the last line of a paragraph is more than one or two words. (A line of only one or two words is called a widow.) Shorten or lengthen a word or phrase earlier in the paragraph to make the lines rewrap and eliminate the widow.

If a second page is necessary, start further down on the first page. Then enough text will move to the second page to make it look balanced.

If there is more than one page, you'll need a heading at the top of each extra page. It should include the recipient's name, the date of the letter, and the page number.

Use 11- or 12-point font size.

Stick with a standard font like Times Roman. It's popular because it's easy to read. Unusual fonts are distracting. Sizes smaller than 10-point are hard to read and sizes larger than 12-point are simply too big for letters.

Take advantage of easy formatting.

Word processing programs have plenty of formats built in. Select the text, click on a command, and the change is complete. Make your ideas jump out with headings, bullets, and numbered lists. Use columns or tables to organize data. Highlight important points with boxes. Experiment with hanging indents and outlines. Allow extra white space so the letter is easier to read.

Just don't overdo the formatting. Too much of it makes the page look busy and will detract from the message. The idea is to make your letter look clean, not clever.

Use templates and style sheets.

You can save time by using templates and styles already built into your word processing program. Templates are pre-set layouts for letters, faxes, memos, reports, and more. Style sheets are pre-set formats for elements like headings, titles, graphics, and tables. Style sheets make use of fonts, italics, boldface, underlining, ruled borders, and columns.

Figure 2.

① **Company Name**
Street Address
City, State Zip
Phone, Fax

MEMORANDUM

② To: From:

Dept./Phone: Dept./Phone

Subject: Date:

④ Body of memo, paragraph 1 xxx x xx xx xxx xx xxxx xxxx xxx xx xxxx xxx xxx xxxx xxx xx xx xxx xx xx x xxxxxxxx xxx xx xx xxxx xxxx xxx xx xxxx xxx xxx xxxx xxx xx xx xxx xx xx x xxx xxxx xxx xxx xxxx xxx xx xxxx xxx xxx xxxxx xxx xx xx xxx xx xx x xxxxxxxx xxx xxx xxxx xx.

Body of memo, paragraph 2 xxx x xx xx xxx xx xxxx xxxx xxx xx xxxx xxx xxx xxxx xxx xx xx xxx xx xx x xxxxxxxx xxx xx xx xxxx xxxx xxx xx xxxx xxx xxx xxxx xxx xx xx xxx xx xx x xxx xxxx xxx xxx xxxx xxx xx xxxx xxx xxx xxxxx xxx xx xx xxx xx xx x xxxxxxxx xxx xxx xxxx xx.

Body of memo, paragraph 3 xxx x xx xx xxx xx xxxx xxxx xxx xx xxxx xxx xxx xxxx xxx xx xx xxx xx xx x xxxxxxxx xxx xx xx xxxx xxxx xxx xx xxxx xx xxx xxxx xxx xx xx xxx xx xx x xxxxx xx xxx xxx xxxx xxx xx xxxx xxx xxx xxxxx xxx xx xx xxx xx xx x xxx xxxx xxx xxx xxxx xx.

⑤ Signature
Signature

⑥ cc: Name
Name

⑦ encl.
ABC/def

Memos

A memo is an informal letter and is usually sent within an organization. Short memos have been largely replaced by in-house e-mails, but memos still have their place. The memo format is excellent for longer messages and reports.

The elements of a memo are similar to those of a letter, but with some variations.

1. Letterhead

The letterhead is at the top of the page. Letterheads for memos are less formal, but still include the company name and address. As with letters, these can be preprinted, scanned into your computer, or available as a template on your word processing program.

2. Heading

The heading includes to, from, subject, and date information. It replaces the addressee's name and address.

The heading can be varied as desired. Follow company guidelines, use a template in your word processor program, or design your own. Two common headings are shown in Figures 2 and 3.

3. Salutation

There is no salutation on a memo.

4. Body of memo

The body of a memo starts two to four lines down from the heading. Single-space within paragraphs; double-space between paragraphs. You can indent if you wish.

Unlike letters, memos do not have to be centered top and bottom. Use the same margins (about 1¼ inches on each side) as for a letter, then let the text end wherever it ends.

5. Closing and signature

No closing or signature is necessary. However, many writers do sign their names or initials at the end of the memo.

6. Copies

If the distribution list is short, position it after *To:* in the heading. For example:

To: John Doe
   cc: Mary Smith
From: Jane Johnson

If the distribution list is long, place it at the end of the memo.

7. Enclosures and initials

These are noted the same way on memos as on letters.

Figure 3.

①
Company Name
Street Address
City, State Zip
Phone, Fax, E-mail

②
MEMO

To:

      cc: ⑥

From:

Date:

Subject:

④
Body of memo, paragraph 1 xxx x xx xx xxx xx xxxx xxxx xxx xx xxxx xxx xxx xxxx xxx xx xx xxx xx xx x xxxxxxx xxx xx xx xxxx xxxx xxx xx xxxx xxx xxx xxxx xxx xx xx xxx xx xx x xxxxxxx xxx xxx xxxx xxx xx xxxx xxx xxx xxxx xxx xx xx xxx xx xx x xxxxxxx xxx xxx xxxx xx.

Body of memo, paragraph 2 xxx x xx xx xxx xx xxxx xxxx xxx xx xxxx xxx xxx xxxx xxx xx xx xxx xx xx x xxxxxxx xxx xx xx xxxx xxxx xxx xx xxxx xxx xxx xxxx xxx xx xx xxx xx xx x xxxxxxx xxx xxx xxxx xxx xx xxxx xxx xxx xxxx xxx xx xx xxx xx xx x xxxxxxx xxx xxx xxxx xx.

Body of memo, paragraph 3 xxx x xx xx xxx xx xxxx xxxx xxx xx xxxx xxx xxx xxxx xxx xx xx xxx xx xx x xxxxxxx xxx xxx xxxx xxx xx xxxx xxx xxx xxxx xxx xx xx xxx xx xx x xxxxxxx xxx xxx xxxx xxx xx xxxx xxx xxx xxxx xxx xx xx xxx xx xx x xxxxxxx xxx xxx xxxx xx.

⑤ *Signature*

⑦
encl.
ABC/def

Figure 4.

Sender's Letterhead
Name, Address, City, State Zip
Phone No., Fax No.

Fax Cover Sheet

No. of pages

Date: _____ (incl. this one): _____

To: _____
    (Name)

    _____
    (Company)

    _____
    (Fax number)

Message:

Fax Correspondence

A facsimile, or fax, machine uses telephone lines to send a digital picture of a document to a second fax machine, which then prints it out. Faxes are easily and quickly transmitted—some systems allow you to send and receive faxes from your computer. Faxes provide an instant method for sending and receiving documents, signatures, forms, and other information.

Fax Cover Sheet

When sending a letter by fax, use a cover sheet (Figure 4). Typically it is a separate piece of paper, but it can also be small and affixed to the upper corner of the first page. It lists the names, phone numbers, and fax numbers of sender and recipient; today's date; and the number of pages being faxed. The Message Section is optional.

This heading can be varied as desired. Follow company guidelines, use a template in your word processor program, or design your own. If the receiving fax is used by only one or a few persons, you might not need a cover sheet. In that case, some writers prefer to add *Via Fax Transmission* to the top of the letter being sent. Other notations are *Fax sent to* [name], *No hard copy to follow*, or *Original sent via U. S. Mail.*

If you are faxing a memo, use the cover sheet heading, but change the title to *Fax Memo.* Add your message to the bottom of the page, and it's ready to go.

Get the Most from Your Faxes

Fax machines save a lot of time. Follow these guidelines to use yours to its best advantage.

Install a separate phone line for your fax machine.

Although one phone line can be used for several purposes, it becomes tedious to switch back and forth every time a fax is sent or received. Most businesses now have separate fax lines, so senders typically insert their documents, dial your number, then walk away. They are not expecting to have to stand by while you switch your phone line over to your fax machine.

Leave your fax machine on.

One of the most important features of a fax machine is that an operator is not required to receive faxes. If the fax machine is turned on, it will automatically answer and receive incoming faxes 24 hours a day. This is significant if you do business with companies in other time zones and other countries.

Use a cover sheet when you send a fax.

In most offices, one fax machine is shared by many people. A cover sheet insures that your document will be given to the proper person right away. Along with the usual to and from information, it should also state how many pages are being faxed (including the cover sheet).

Faxed signatures are generally accepted as legally binding.

If both parties agree, faxed signatures can save lots of time. The first person signs a contract, then faxes it to the second. The receiver signs the fax, then faxes it back. Now both parties have a signed contract for their files, so the work can begin. If you choose to follow up with a hard copy, remember that this is merely a formality. The faxed signatures are binding.

Fine print, detailed art, and small handwriting do not fax well.

Faxed documents do not have the same quality as the originals. If you know ahead of time your document will be faxed, avoid small type and fancy fonts or your fax may be illegible to your reader when it is eventually received.

If you are designing a form that users will fill out with pen and ink, allow plenty of space. You want to be sure the information will be legible after it is faxed.

Be aware of security issues.

Think twice before transmitting sensitive information via fax. If the wrong number is dialed, the fax will be sent to the wrong company. Also, one fax machine is typically shared by an entire department or office, so a fax might be read by several people before it ends up on the intended recipient's desk.

E-Mail

E-mail, or electronic mail, has become the first choice for interoffice correspondence. You can originate a message or respond to incoming e-mail very quickly—in some instances e-mail is more efficient than voice mail. You can answer a query as soon as you read it, or you can print it out and look at it later, perhaps while commuting or traveling. For example, e-mail is great for coordinating meetings: You can quickly remind participants of the time and place, send the agenda in advance, then let everyone review minutes and decisions afterward. If there are any discrepancies or misunderstandings, you'll be told right away.

E-mail tends to be informal. Most users are willing to accept typos and other mistakes in order to send a fast message or get a speedy reply. But take care, because too many errors will distract the reader and divert attention from your message.

E-mail can also be overwhelming. It's not unusual for some people to receive 70 or more e-mail messages every business day. Although you can respond instantly, you still have to make a decision about each one—answer now, answer later, read and remember, read and forget, and on and on. There is a lot of pressure just to keep up.

Get the Most from Your E-mail

E-mail can be a very powerful tool. Here are some suggestions to make your e-mail messages more effective.

Limit each e-mail message to one topic.

If your e-mail message addresses only one topic, your recipient can act on it, then go to the next message. The action might be making a phone call, writing a memo, or simply making mental note of the information you provided and filing your message. In any case, your recipient can respond and be done. If your e-mail message covers several topics, a less important issue might be forgotten or overlooked.

Limit the length of an e-mail message to one screen.

Business e-mail is excellent for brief queries and information messages. With a few keystrokes, recipients can reply, quickly crossing off one more item from their "to do" lists.

If you have lots to say, it's better to send a letter or memo, then send an e-mail message that summarizes your report or at least says it's on the way. Many businesspeople report that they prefer not to scroll through several screens of text. If the information is part of an ongoing business deal, they will probably print it out anyway.

Avoid putting words or phrases in capitals.

Some writers use capital letters to get your attention. The use of capitals in the electronic environment means the writer is SHOUTING at you. Shouting is considered rude, whether in person or in print.

SOME WRITERS LIKE TO TYPE IN ALL CAPS SO THEY DON'T HAVE TO USE A SHIFT KEY. Unfortunately, a string of capital letters is hard to read. Your eye can scan upper- and lower-case text much more quickly than it can scan all caps. Solve this problem by learning to type.

Capitals are also used as shorthand for commonly used phrases. Two common business acronyms are FYI (for your information) and ASAP (as soon as possible). More casual acronyms, such as BTY (by the way), TTFN (ta ta for now), IMHO (in my humble opinion), and ROFL (rolling on the floor laughing), are inappropriate for business correspondence.

Use italics appropriately.

Titles of books, plays, movies, newspapers, and magazines should be in italics. Using italics for emphasis can be condescending. Your reader doesn't need a *signpost* to get the point.

Use standard punctuation.

"Cute" punctuation (♥ or *XOXO*) is inappropriate for business e-mail messages. Save the smiles—:)—and frowns—: (—and winks —;)—for personal correspondence.

Learn to spell.

Shoddy spelling distracts the reader and reflects poorly on you. Find out if your mail editor has a spell checker. If it does, use it, then quickly proofread. Readers tend to accept the occasional typo if they know you were in a hurry, but a message with too many errors is unprofessional.

Save fancy formatting for letters.

Although it is prudent to use all of your computer's features to create a good-looking e-mail message, remember that complicated files might not transfer with their original formatting. On-line programs vary, and some systems may not transmit graphics or unusual fonts. Your very important and beautifully formatted message may appear as gibberish on the recipient's computer. If you are unsure, a plain text message is the best way to go.

Avoid long message threads.

One of the advantages of e-mail is the ability to forward a message, adding a brief comment of your own. Any number of people can do this, each adding to the thread of the message.

The problem is that message threads quickly become unwieldy. The last comment added is at the top of the thread; the original message is at the bottom. Headers are also likely to be included throughout; these too are lengthy and can interrupt a reader's train of thought as he or she pages through screen after screen, trying to follow the thread.

As a rule of thumb, once a thread contains three or more messages, it is better to start a new one. If the document is easy to read, you're likely to get a more thoughtful response.

Be aware of security issues.

Remember that e-mail messages can—and do—go astray in cyberspace. You might push the wrong button, or your computer thinks you did. An assistant or coworker might be checking e-mail for an intended recipient who is out of the office.

Sensitive information should never be transmitted through e-mail unless your company uses a well-secured system. Skilled hackers can break into e-mail accounts—and they will if they have reason to believe the information is valuable.

Store paperless mail in paperless files.

E-mail is paperless, so use it to your advantage. Messages can be read, filed, and disposed of at the touch of a button. Learning how to file each e-mail message in the proper electronic file will save time and disk space.

Resist the temptation to print out every single e-mail message. Instead, learn to read e-mail on your computer screen. Print out only those messages that you plan to read later or that are important enough to require a hard copy backup in your regular files. Other than official documents or those with forms to be filled out (a pen might be faster than moving a cursor around), most e-mails can remain paperless.

Read the manual.

Invest some time to learn how your e-mail system works. Most systems allow for on-line address books, group mailings, auto formatting, spell checking, and more. Spending an hour or more perusing your manual will save you hundreds of hours in the future. Try out a few options by sending test files to an understanding friend or coworker.

Voice Mail

Voice mail is an important component of today's business communication. It's almost, but not quite, a written message: The caller might make a quick note before dialing, and the listener might write down an important fact while playing back the message.

Many businesspeople receive 40 or more voice messages each day, so long and chatty messages are not likely to be appreciated. In fact, your listener might press a button and move on to the next message, assuming that you have nothing important to say.

Get the Most from Your Voice Mail

Think of voice mail as though it were a written communication. You want your message to make sense so that you will get the response you want. Here are some suggestions that may help.

Organize your thoughts before you dial.

Jot down a few notes or make a quick list so your message is complete. Listeners prefer short, organized messages. No one has time to listen to long pauses, ahs, uhs, and "Oh, I forgot to tell you...."

Once you're connected, get to the point right away. "I'm calling to tell you that XYZ Corp. is insisting on an insurance codicil in the contract."

Speak slowly and clearly.

Make it easy for your listener to understand you. Clear your throat and swallow that last bite of ham sandwich before you dial.

If your listener will need to write something down, speak slowly. If the information is important, repeat it. For example, repeat airline flight numbers and arrival or departure times, invoice numbers, street addresses, phone numbers, hotel and rental car data, and the like.

Identify yourself.

"Hi, it's me," isn't enough identification. The listener might not recognize your voice at all. "Hi, it's Bob," is better, but your listener still might have to guess—Which Bob? Bob who? "Hi, it's Bob Jones at ABC Corp." is best because there's no conjecture involved.

Remember to leave your phone number, too. It's possible your listener is picking up calls from a remote location and doesn't have your phone number handy. You may also want to remind the listener of your fax number, business hours, etc., but be careful not to bore your listener with unwanted information.

Leave brief messages—one minute or less.

If your message is longer than one minute, it's too long. If you have lots to say, put it in writing and send a fax or e-mail message.

Assume that you probably don't have your listener's undivided attention. People tend to do a second task while they are playing back voice messages. They go through their in-boxes, read, straighten up their desks, file papers, sip sodas, wave at friends and coworkers walking by their cubicles. If they have car phones, they might play back messages while driving.

Many phones also have a "jump forward" option, so if you're blathering on, your listener might move to the next call without listening to your complete message. State the important part of your message first, then add the details. Listening to voice messages takes time, so be thoughtful—make your point and hang up.

If you want a specific response, say so. Give a reason, and you're more likely to get a response. "If this is okay with you, let me know. I need your authorization before I can proceed."

Be aware of security issues.

Voice mail is not private. Your message can be played back on a speaker phone while others are in the room. Conversations on cordless phones can be picked up with radio equipment. If the person you called is out of the office, an assistant or coworker can listen to those messages—presumably with permission.

Personal, private messages should always be delivered in person and in private.

Be prepared to call again.

Even though you left a message asking for a return call, the responsibility for making contact is still yours. If you have urgent business, keep calling.

Leave another voice message. Speak with another person who can pass along your message or who can suggest the best time to try again. Page the person through a company operator. Be persistent until you make contact.

Keep a log of phone calls.

Voice mail also becomes an oral log of what happened—who said what, what was decided, what the next step is. If your system permits, you can archive especially vital or sensitive messages.

Your business may require that you keep an elaborate contact management sheet. If not, a log sheet taped to your desk will work fine. The point is to keep a written record. Listing incoming and outgoing calls helps you keep track of whom you called, who called you, whether you spoke in person or via voice mail, and what you need to do. You can use this information to stay organized, ensure you have the right information available, and remind yourself when you last contacted a customer.

Getting Words on Paper

Everyone at some time has looked at a plain piece of paper or a blank computer screen, hoping a few well-chosen and brilliant words would magically appear. You start to write or type and those first words seem trite, stilted, unfocused, even nonsensical. So you rip up the paper, erase, cross out, start over. After a few more false starts, your pen is still, your fingers refuse to move, and your mind is full of terror. You have a full-blown case of writer's block.

Remember that writing is a skill, like typing or standing up on water skis. It takes practice. The more you write, the easier it gets, and the better your writing will be. Here are some suggestions that will help you get started.

Use stream-of-consciousness writing.

Pretend you are talking and write down what you would say if the person were sitting across from your desk. The goal is to get everything down on paper, then revise it later. It's often easier to re-work, rewrite, and reorganize than it is to write that first draft. If you have someone to help you, dictate the letter first, then rewrite it using the transcription as your first draft.

Make a brief outline.

List the important points and include any key phrases that come to mind. Use this as a guideline for starting to write. Stick to your outline so you know what to say next. Chances are, your writing will be more focused and on track. This is also a good method to use if you are dictating.

Think in terms of three paragraphs.

If you're really stuck, this approach might help. Start by referring to a previous contact: "your letter of September 6," "our phone conversation of yesterday afternoon," "this morning's meeting." If this is a new contact, offer a reason why you're writing: "applying for the job in Sunday's *Gazette*," "special offer," "introduce myself."

Get your point across in the middle paragraph. It can be a list, an explanation, a recommendation, a sales pitch, or whatever you're saying to the recipient.

Use the last paragraph to end the letter with a thank you or a timetable for action—"look forward to hearing from you," "thanks again for your help," "please let me know by Friday."

Remember that shorter is better.

Shorter words, sentences, and paragraphs are easier to read—and less likely to be misread. Stick to one subject per letter or memo. Even if you're writing to the same person, write a separate letter to address each topic. That makes record keeping and follow-up easier for both writer and reader.

Be willing to revise.

Sometimes it is necessary to rewrite a sentence or paragraph. Make sure that you said what you really meant to say. Read it aloud and listen to your words. Rewrite anything that isn't clear or might be misunderstood.

Reward yourself for getting it done.

Do the hardest writing early in the day when you're fresh. When you're finished and the report is ready to send, do something positive for yourself. Stretch, walk around the block, meet a friend after work for racquetball, or call your significant other and make a date to see a movie.

Last but not least...

Think about the context in which your communication will be received. Will the recipient be reading your letter at the office first thing in the morning or on the commuter train at the end of the day? Will your voice message be picked up by the intended recipient or an assistant? Will the e-mail message be read at work, at home, or somewhere else? While many of these factors will be out of your control, some consideration on your part might make a difference.

Be aware of sensitive topics that may have legal ramifications. You should consult your attorney or legal department when dealing with issues such as employee performance, changes to a contract, and financial negotiations. Make sure you're in compliance with company policy. If you're not sure about something, ask.

Be polite. If you're annoyed or frustrated with the situation at hand, wait until the emotion subsides. The problem will wait for you, so deal with it later today or tomorrow when you're in a better frame of mind. Remember that a thoughtful letter promotes understanding and cooperation. Take whatever time you need to respond with courtesy and decency to your business associates, friends, and fellow workers.

Part II

Accept Civic Position

Situation   *Many businesspeople contribute to their communities by serving in unpaid civic positions. Their expertise is a great asset to these organizations, and it is often considered an honor to be asked to participate.*

The Letter   Dear Arts Council:

I was very pleased to receive the letter announcing my appointment to the Arts Council board of directors. Thank you for your vote of confidence. The Arts Council is a most prestigious organization in this community, and I hope that I can make a positive contribution.

Thank you again for this honor. I look forward to seeing you on the afternoon of September 4, Meeting Room A, Town Hall.

Sincerely,

Accept Membership

Situation   *This writer is accepting an invitation to join a civic organization. The letter is brief, but conveys the writer's enthusiasm.*

The Letter   Dear Name:

Thank you for your letter of July 18. I am honored to accept your invitation to join your executive board.

I am well aware of the positive impact your organization has on this community, and I will do my best to contribute to your continuing efforts.

Thank you again for this honor. I look forward to meeting the other members of the board at the August meeting.

Sincerely,

Accept Social Invitation

Situation   *Your response should match the invitation. If the invitation was a written one, reply in writing to say whether or not you'll be there. If you can't accept, you don't have to give a reason, though it's okay if you do. If you're planning to attend, restate the date and time to show you understand the plans.*

The Letter   Dear Name:

Dave and I will be at your house at 7 p.m. sharp next Friday, the 24th. We won't say a word, because we too want Mary to be surprised.

We're excited about the festivities. It promises to be fun.

Best wishes,

Accept Speaking Engagement

Situation   *This writer is agreeing to be a guest speaker. The letter also notifies the recipient that certain audiovisual equipment will be needed. If the speaker is charging a fee, a contract would most likely be enclosed.*

The Letter   Dear Name:

I am happy to accept your invitation to be the keynote speaker at your annual symposium on January 15th. I will plan to arrive at the airport early that morning and leave after the luncheon speech. Per your request, I am enclosing a photograph and sample flyer that you are welcome to use to help promote your symposium.

Please reserve audiovisual equipment with the conference center ahead of time. I will need a microphone, overhead projector, and screen. A lectern with a microphone will be acceptable, but I prefer a clip-on, cord-free mike so that I can move around the room.

Thank you again for this honor. I am looking forward to meeting everyone there.

Sincerely,

Accept Speaking Engagement

Situation

This writer uses one letter to accomplish three things—accept an invitation, forward a contract, and list requirements for the workshop.

The Letter

Dear Name:

Thank you for your kind invitation to be the guest speaker at your organization's May meeting. I am happy to do so.

Per your request, I will give a lecture and slide show in the morning and present a workshop in the afternoon. The workshop is limited to twenty participants. We'll need long tables (6 ft x 2 ft) for the workshop, one per participant plus two additional ones for my use.

I am enclosing a contract for your convenience. Please note that 25% of the lecture and workshop fees are payable upon signing. The remainder, including transportation costs, can be paid at the conclusion of the workshop. As soon as the contract is returned, I will have my travel agent book the trip to take advantage of the lowest possible airfare.

Thanks again for the invitation. I look forward to meeting you and working with your group.

Sincerely,

Account Credited

Situation   *It is easy to write a letter that will please the recipient. This letter tells the customer that money was credited to an account.*

The Letter   Dear Name:

Thank you for contacting us regarding your recent bill. After investigating this matter thoroughly, I am pleased to tell you that we are issuing a credit to you in the amount of $150. This credit will appear on your October statement.

Thank you for bringing this matter to our attention. We are pleased that we were able to be of service. If you have any other questions, please call one of our customer service agents at (123) 456-7890.

Sincerely,

Account Status Changed

Situation   *This customer has qualified for VIP status. The letter outlines the new benefits.*

The Letter   Dear Name:

We are pleased to inform you that your account has been changed to Preferred Customer status. As a Preferred Customer you will receive a 20% discount on all regularly priced items. In addition, your orders will be sent second-day air at no extra charge to you.

Your name has been added to our mailing list and you will be receiving notices of special sales. You will also be receiving quarterly updates of our catalog.

Please call our customer representative if you have any questions or require any special orders. We look forward to serving you.

Sincerely,

Acknowledge Cancellation of Service

Situation

Acknowledging canceled service is good practice in case the business received erroneous notification. The acknowledgment letter can also set the stage for winning the customer back at a later date.

The Letter

Dear Cardholder:

We received your letter of June 4 and have canceled your account as you requested. If you still have your account card, be sure to cut it in half to destroy it.

Whenever you decide to reopen this account, simply contact our customer service department between the hours of 6 a.m. and midnight, Monday through Saturday.

We hope that we will be able to serve you again in the future.

Sincerely,

Acknowledge Error

Situation   *A letter acknowledging an error should also include fixing the error. This letter encloses a revised statement to show that the correction was made.*

The Letter   Dear Name:

Thanks for the fax regarding the first quarter inventory statement. You are right—the shipment from XYZ Supplies of 65,000 units arrived in February, not March. A corrected inventory statement is attached for your files.

Just a reminder: If you have any other corrections, I will need them before noon on Friday.

Thanks again for bringing this to my attention.

Best regards,

Acknowledge First Order

Situation   *First orders are sometimes small, but they are likely to be stepping stones to larger orders. It is reasonable to assume that the small order is a test to see how well your company will handle this new account. Thus, every order deserves attention and care. Show your appreciation by acknowledging it.*

The Letter   Dear Name:

Thank you for your December 17th order for connector components. I checked with our warehouse superintendent and found out that your order is being quality checked this afternoon, so it should arrive at your Phoenix facility a day or two ahead of schedule.

We appreciate your business and look forward to continuing to supply you with the most reliable components in the industry.

Cordially,

Acknowledge Receipt

Situation   *This letter acknowledges receipt of an application, but offers no encouragement.*

The Letter   Dear Name:

Thank you for letter and resume of April 18th. I have forwarded your resume to the proper department where it will be reviewed.

As you may know, we are considering many candidates. We will be in touch with you if we decide to pursue your application further.

Thank you for your interest in our company.

Sincerely,

Additional Data Needed

Situation   *Putting together elaborate computer systems can be arduous because of the amount of detailed information required. Once the system is operational, however, keeping the database up to date is a relatively straightforward task.*

The Letter   Dear Name:

We are now in the final stages of setting up the standardized system for your purchasing and inventory control procedures.

The following information is still outstanding:

1. List of outlet locations, including store names and addresses.

2. Key contact at each location, including names and titles.

Thanks for your prompt attention to this matter.

Sincerely,

Advertising Promotion

Situation   *This writer is sending materials to a business partner to show that a job was completed. Although a cover letter might not have been necessary, it provides an opportunity for the writer to say thank you.*

The Letter   Dear Name:

Enclosed are copies of the print ads that will be appearing in the regional newspapers in this area during the next month. The first one appeared in last Sunday's paper and orders are already coming in. This is the major advertising campaign for this season.

Thank you for your monetary support in this co-op promotional effort. Your support is greatly appreciated, and we are confident this promotion will yield positive sales results.

Sincerely,

Agenda

Situation

An agenda lists topics for discussion and the order in which they will be addressed. An agenda helps keep a meeting on track. When participants receive the agenda in advance, they can prepare any necessary materials ahead of time. They can also request that additional items of importance be added to the agenda.

The Letter

The next regular meeting of the Order Fulfillment Group will be Tuesday, March 14 at 9:30 a.m. in conference room C.

AGENDA

<u>Status Reports</u>

    Industrial Sales—John

    Retail Sales—Dick

    Customer Service—Mary

    Warehouse—Jane

    Shipping—Bill

    Purchasing—Ed

<u>New Business</u>

    Possible delivery service slowdown/strike

Please make your status reports brief. Most of our meeting will be focused on readiness plans in case the threatened transportation strike comes to pass.

Agenda Item

Situation   *This manager has been studying one aspect of the business and wants to see improvement in this area. A report is forwarded and recipients are asked to have suggestions ready.*

The Letter   The attached graph shows the accuracy with which customer service fulfills orders. During our busy winter season, there is an increase in incomplete and late orders. Although this is to be expected, it is still not acceptable. What is worrisome, however, is that the percentage of late orders has jumped from 38% to 53%.

At the next management meeting, let's address what we can do now to minimize this problem. To improve this situation, we need to look at forecasting, inventory control, and increased activities with new products and programs.

Order fulfillment will be on next month's agenda, so let's start thinking about solutions now.

Agenda Overview

Situation

Most business meetings are more productive if participants prepare in advance. This letter is quite specific about meeting arrangements and what needs to be done in advance.

The Letter

Dear Name:

Attached is the agenda for your visit to Dallas next month. Plan to arrive by noon on August 15 and depart the morning of August 17.

In order to use our time together to its fullest advantage, I have asked everyone involved to review all the information regarding XYZ Company. I ask that you come prepared to discuss each agenda item from XYZ's perspective. I anticipate that our meetings will resolve tactical questions and problems, so that when we meet the following week we can deal with strategic issues.

This agenda is certainly flexible, so give me a call if I have overlooked anything. I think our meeting next month promises to be a productive one.

Sincerely,

Announce New Business

Situation

Sales letters are really advertisements. They are written to sell a service, a product, or an idea. You can catch the reader's eye with fancy type and bright colors, but in the end it's your words that will convince the reader to do business with you. A good sales letter doesn't exaggerate or distort; it simply talks about what you have to sell. Think about what you say when you talk to your customers, then put those words in a letter format.

The Letter

Dear Name:

Want to ship furniture to your son's new apartment? Need to send a holiday package to a friend in Europe? Need some color copies? Stamps?

There's a new way to take care of your mailing and shipping needs—<u>Packages and More, Inc.</u>

We specialize in packing any size item—from household furnishings to wedding rings. Then we'll ship it for you to arrive whenever you want. Most items can be delivered the next business day—we'll even send a messenger to hand-carry it if necessary. Large domestic shipments that go by truck or rail might take a bit longer, but even those shipments will probably arrive the same week. Call for information on foreign shipments—delivery guarantees vary from one country to another.

Our office and main shipping depot are at 100 E. Higgins Road, just a block south of the Sangamon County railroad station. We have big and little boxes, tape, bubble wrap, and more to make your packing and shipping fast and easy. Bring your packages to us, or give us a call and we'll pick up your shipment at your business or residence.

We can also help you with your office needs in our new facility. We have copiers, collators, copy paper in many colors, and envelopes and mailers in all sizes.

To show our appreciation, we're offering a 20% discount on your next shipment and a 10% discount on color copies for the rest of this month.

We're here to help, so give us a call or stop by. Our doors are open from 8 a.m. to 8 p.m. during the week and 9 a.m. to 4 p.m. on weekends.

Sincerely,

Announce Training Classes

Situation

Part of introducing or upgrading a company computer system is teaching employees how to use it. Continuing education courses of this nature can boost morale as well as productivity.

The Letter

Dear Name:

Training classes on the new order fulfillment system are about to begin. We want all shift supervisors to be the first to learn how to use this new system. It gives us on-line access to the major shipping and freight companies with whom we have contracts.

The first class will be held Monday at 9 a.m. in the annex at 102 Main Street. The training session will last approximately 1½ hours and will start on time. Bring a note pad and pencil. We'll have coffee and doughnuts for you at the break.

If you need to reschedule, give me a call.

Sincerely,

Announcement of Acquisition

Situation

When one company purchases another, it announces its newest acquisition. Employees, however, are more likely to be worried about how this acquisition will affect their jobs. This announcement to employees attempts to address their concerns. The first paragraph can also be used as part of a press release.

The Letter

Today KAS Construction Group announces their acquisition of Quality Planing, a company specializing in planing roads for resurfacing and patching. "Quality Planing will benefit the entire group," said owner Stephen Smith, "and will help KAS Construction continue its growth as a full-service road construction and engineering firm. We feel that this acquisition is beneficial to all of our employees because it qualifies KAS Construction to bid on and accept government contracts. These are usually larger jobs and continue throughout the year." Other companies owned by KAS include QRS Asphalt and XYZ Material Company. Each company in the KAS Construction Group will continue to operate under its original name.

This new acquisition will bring about the following changes: Bob Kelly will be in charge of bids and estimates for all KAS companies. Richard Davis has been promoted from site foreman to general superintendent. Bing Wagner and Rose Witten are now promoted to site foremen. Larry Johnson will continue as head engineer; Molly Matheson has been promoted to assistant engineer.

There will be some additional restructuring as well. Those whose jobs are immediately affected have already been notified and are working with Human Resources at this time. All employees who will be terminated due to this restructuring will continue to receive their salaries through August 1, and their medical and hospitalization coverage will continue through the end of the year.

We appreciate all of our employees' continued cooperation as we work through this transition period.

Apology to Customer

Situation   *This brief letter can do a great deal to soothe the feelings of an irritated customer. The writer simply admits there was an error and encloses proof that the matter was corrected.*

The Letter   Dear Name:

You're right. We made a mistake.

You were overcharged on invoice A-123 by $50.21. We have credited your account for this amount, and a corrected statement is attached for your records.

Thanks for bringing this to our attention.

Sincerely,

Apology to Customer

Situation   *An apology letter can do more than express regret—it can let the customer know that the complaint was valid and steps are being taken to see that it does not happen again.*

The Letter   Dear Name:

Thank you for your letter of October 3 describing the problems you have been having with XYZ. I appreciate your candor and must agree that we are not managing our co-op program very well. Please accept my sincere apologies.

We are not taking your dissatisfaction lightly. In fact, your letter has been forwarded to several key people in our organization, including our president. We are already working to improve our internal process, and I hope you will bear with us as we develop a better approach to handling specific issues that arise with this program.

Sincerely,

Application Follow-Up

Situation   *When applying for a job, it is important to be available to potential employers. Otherwise they might assume you are not interested after all.*

The Letter   Dear Name:

We have reviewed your application for employment and would like to speak with you further. However, we have been unable to reach you by phone.

We would appreciate your contacting us. If we do not hear from you by the 18th, we will assume that you are not interested in pursuing this matter further.

Sincerely,

Apply for Credit Account

Situation   *To open a business credit account, the customer typically completes an application form and submits whatever information is required. This letter accompanies the application.*

The Letter   Dear Name:

I would like to establish an open account with your firm. To that end, I am returning the completed application and three credit references. I have also enclosed our Dun & Bradstreet rating for your records.

I am confident this information will meet with your approval, and I am looking forward to doing business with you.

My first order is ready to go and I will send it in as soon as I hear from your credit department.

Sincerely,

Appreciation Letter

Situation

Letters of appreciation are important. Successes in business are often the result of teamwork. You may have been the team leader, but it was the combined efforts of several individuals that brought about the success. Take time to let team members know you are aware of their contributions.

The Letter

Dear Name:

I want to tell you again how much I appreciated your help on the XYZ account. Your careful background research put us on the right track from the very beginning as we mapped out the overall advertising campaign. Your attention to detail throughout was vital to our success.

Our team is superior because of people like you. Thanks again for your contribution.

Best regards,

Appreciation Letter

Situation   *Take time to praise a fellow worker. This letter says thank you and expresses appreciation for someone who went the extra mile.*

The Letter   Dear Name:

I would like to recognize John Doe in your department for being especially helpful as we prepare for this year's vendor show. John has helped us with rush requirements, making an effort to arrange for delivery of equipment after the cut-off time. He has demonstrated grace under pressure during these preparations.

Thanks to his help, we are better prepared than ever, and we expect to have a much better show.

Sincerely,

Approval Needed

Situation

When asking for authorization or approval, be sure to include all information needed for the decision. This letter makes a recommendation and includes costs.

The Letter

Dear Name:

At last year's sales meeting, we discussed the possibility of having a courtesy suite for customers at the Albuquerque trade show.

I recommend that we rent a small banquet room for the three evenings of the show and provide snacks and drinks for customers. Based on previous attendance records, we will probably have about 75 to 100 visitors each evening. A detailed cost breakdown is attached.

I would like to finalize arrangements, but I need your okay.

Sincerely,

Authorization

━━━━━━━━━━━

Situation   *This is a letter of authorization to proceed as discussed. The writer also acknowledges the work that the recipient has done to correct this problem.*

The Letter   Dear Name:

This is to authorize you to use corrugated cardboard dividers in the cartons used to pack fine china. These will replace the chipboard dividers now being used.

Thanks again for all of your efforts on this matter. This change will reduce china breakage at no cost to us. It should be easy to implement since the outer carton dimensions remain the same.

You've really done a great job. Keep up the good work!

Sincerely,

Award Announcement

Situation

Businesses need good employees. Recognizing those whose work is exemplary is important because it helps build company morale. Employees at all levels like to know that their hard work is noticed and appreciated.

The Letter

XYZ Corporation is proud to announce that John Doe has been named the Employee of the Year in recognition of his outstanding service to his customers. Mr. Doe's commitment to each of his customers exemplifies the highest standards of personal and professional service.

Mr. Doe has been an employee of XYZ for five years. He is an account supervisor in Computerized Document Management. Please join us in congratulating him on this well-deserved honor.

"Be Considerate" Notice

Situation   *Common-use areas are utilized by many people. These areas often have signs posted near the entrances reminding users to be considerate of others who follow.*

The Letter   The conference room is available to all, but we need your help in keeping it tidy for the next group that uses it.

      A. Take your papers and other belongings with you. Anything left behind might be thrown away.

      B. Turn off everything—coffee pot, baseboard heater, and lights.

      C. Shut the door.

Thank you for following these ABCs.

Bid Cover Letter

Situation

This cover letter reminds the recipient that revisions to the original specifications will probably affect the prices quoted.

The Letter

Dear Name:

Attached is our bid 123-45 for the XYZ project.

This bid assumes that if it is granted, all parties will work together to develop a mutually agreeable construction schedule. This bid is also based on information provided at this time. Any revisions required at a later date will be subject to price review at that time. We reserve the right to withdraw this bid if it is not accepted within 45 days.

Thank you for giving us this opportunity. We look forward to hearing from you.

Sincerely,

Bid Proposal

Situation *This letter bids on a job. It describes the project and includes costs.*

The Letter Dear Name:

We propose to furnish labor and materials for the following work at the new XYZ office.

Install a 6 ft × 10 ft partition from the floor to the underside of the roof deck in order to separate the space in units 3 and 4. The wall will have sound attenuation blankets. Each side will be covered with $5/_8$-inch drywall and taped.

Our price for performing this work is $3,467. A detailed cost breakdown is attached. As soon as we have your approval, we can begin work on this job for you.

Sincerely,

Bid Request

Situation

Many corporations and government agencies ask specialist businesses to bid on various projects. Invitations to bid are similar to this one.

The Letter

Dear Name:

XYZ Corporation is now accepting bids for landscaping services. This bid is in two parts; you may bid on one or both parts.

Part I is to landscape the corporate headquarters as shown on the attached design. Your bid should include prices for labor plus trees, shrubs, and other plantings as shown. Part II is for regular maintenance of corporate grounds. Bids should include a monthly price for routine maintenance and what that would include, e.g., mowing, pruning, raking. Detailed specifications are available for inspection in this office.

Bids should be addressed to Plant Manager and must be received no later than Friday, December 20th by the close of business. The contract for Part I will be awarded on January 15th. The contract for Part II will be awarded on February 1 and will be for a period of two years.

If you have any questions regarding this project, please contact this office.

Sincerely,

Billing Error

Situation   *Writing a letter to document a billing error is worth the few minutes it takes. Putting the problem in writing makes it easier for the company to correct, especially if it takes more than one person to handle the problem.*

The Letter   Dear Name:

Enclosed is my check for $44.50 in payment of invoice 2345 dated August 26, 19xx.

Note that this invoice also includes a California-to-Oregon delivery for $11.50 which was billed to this account in error. Please re-bill to the proper sender, XYZ Systems in Los Angeles, California.

Thank you for your assistance in this matter.

Sincerely,

Billing Instructions

Situation

This letter accompanies a purchase order. Hopefully the supplier will read it carefully because it explains that merchandise and invoices should be sent to separate addresses.

The Letter

Dear Name:

Enclosed is our purchase order A-1234 for four styles of dress shoes in the sizes specified.

Merchandise should be drop-shipped directly to individual stores; packing slips and copies of the invoice should be enclosed with each drop shipment.

Please set up your billing procedures so that all invoices for the merchandise are sent to our corporate accounts payable office. Invoicing this office directly will save time and speed up your payment.

We are pleased to be carrying your products and look forward to a mutually rewarding business relationship.

Sincerely,

Budget Payment Plan

Situation   *Businesses with seasonal cost fluctuations find it pays to prorate customer bills over an extended period. Customers can budget better and are less likely to fall behind on payments during high-usage months.*

The Letter   Dear Name:

We are pleased to offer a new service to make it easier to pay your heating bill.

Using your last year's usage as a guideline, we will prorate your estimated annual usage, then divide your bill into twelve equal payments. This makes your monthly bill easier to handle and budget. Your account will be reviewed every six months to make any necessary adjustments. As long as your monthly bill is paid on time, there is no interest charge for this service.

To make it even easier, you can authorize us to deduct payment automatically from your checking account each month. You save on postage and avoid service charges on late payments. We'll send you a monthly statement for your records.

If you would like to take advantage of this new service, please give us a call. We look forward to serving you.

Sincerely,

Building Security

Situation   *Many companies have found it necessary to restrict access to their buildings in order to protect employees and company property. This business has installed door locks that can be accessed with a swipe card.*

The Letter   Dear Name:

A new security system has been installed at each entrance of each building. Doors can be opened from the outside only with a swipe card. The cards are programmed individually. Not every card will open every door.

Every employee is issued his or her own card. Yours is attached to the bottom of this notice. Take care of it because replacement cards cost $10 each.

If you have any questions or lose your card, call John Doe, ext. 123.

Business for Sale

Situation   *The seller wishes to remain anonymous except to serious buyers. News of an impending sale could affect employee morale as well as profits.*

The Letter   Dear Name:

As a business broker I represent a business that is currently for sale. This company has been in business for more than 15 years and has sales of approximately $1.5 million.

Because most of their products and channels for marketing appear to be complementary with yours, I thought you might be interested in acquiring the company. Please call me if you would like additional information about this business opportunity.

Thank you for your consideration.

Sincerely,

Business Referral

Situation

When a customer recommends your products or services to an associate, that is a business lead worth pursuing. The best advertising any business has is word of mouth.

The Letter

Dear Name:

Ron Jones suggested that I get in touch with you regarding industrial lifting equipment. Our company deals in material handling and shop equipment—both new and reconditioned. We specialize in platform trucks, fork lifts, pallet racks, and conveyors.

With the proper equipment you can reduce injuries in your warehouse and increase productivity by as much as 35%. Many of our customers find that the right equipment can pay for itself within three to six months. We offer free consulting to help you choose the equipment that will allow your materials to be handled at the safest working height for the operator.

We invite you to visit our showroom and test some of our equipment yourself. I'll give you a call early next week to set up a convenient time.

Cordially,

Business Referral

Situation

One of the best ways to keep customers is to become an advocate for them. If you like what they do, recommend their products and services to others. Whenever you help a client's business grow, you'll be remembered as a friend. In return, perhaps they will recommend you too.

The Letter

Dear Name:

I wanted to pass along some information that might prove useful.

XYZ Lighting is taking a serious look at how they can improve their sales in the industrial market. I mentioned your line of commercial fixtures designed for energy conservation. Sheila Graver, West Coast regional sales manager, was very interested and would like more information. I'm enclosing her business card so you can get in touch with her.

Hope this turns out to be a viable lead. It certainly sounded to me like your products are what they're looking for.

Sincerely,

Cancel Credit Card

Situation   *To cancel a service, a long letter is unnecessary. Simply put your cancellation notice in writing. The writer includes other pertinent information.*

The Letter   Dear Credit Card Company:

Enclosed is payment in full for account #54321.

Please cancel this account, effective immediately. I am the only cardholder on the account. I have destroyed the card by cutting it in half.

Thank you.

Sincerely,

Change in Job Requirements

Situation   *This letter acknowledges an application and explains that the job parameters have changed.*

The Letter   Dear Name:

We have received and reviewed your resume for our part-time position for administrative assistant.

We were delayed in filling this position because the person in the job was able to stay a few weeks longer than originally planned. After reevaluating our staffing needs, we have decided that we need a full-time instead of a part-time assistant.

If you are still interested in this position as a full-time employee, please contact me by the end of next week.

Yours truly,

Character Reference

Situation   *Writing a reference letter takes serious thought. You want to convey factual information as well as support the person in his or her application. If you are unable to write a positive letter in good conscience, say no when the applicant asks you for an endorsement.*

The Letter   Dear Name:

It is with great pleasure that I recommend John Doe. I have known him for twenty years.

John has always displayed a high degree of integrity, responsibility, and ambition. He is definitely a leader rather than a follower. In addition to his excellent scholastic accomplishments, he has proven his leadership ability by organizing a hockey league in North Dakota to provide young people an opportunity to compete and learn good sportsmanship.

He is also a most dependable team player. His good judgment and mature outlook ensure a logical and practical approach to his endeavors.

Mr. Doe would be an asset to any organization, and I am happy to give him my wholehearted endorsement.

Sincerely,

Clarification of Information

Situation   *This letter clarifies information for a customer. Although a phone call might have sufficed, a letter gives the customer a reference in case the question comes up again.*

The Letter   Dear Name:

Thanks for the information you forwarded. Let me clarify the item number that we use in our catalog.

We use a four-digit item number followed by a dash and a three-digit alpha suffix, for example, 1234-ABC. The alpha code identifies the supplier and the catalog in which the item appears. The number code stays the same, but the alpha code changes with different catalogs and promotions so that we can track how various items are selling.

I hope this answers your questions.

Sincerely,

Close an Open Account

Situation

When customers continually pay their bills late, it may become necessary to close those accounts. This letter changes a customer's account status from credit to cash.

The Letter

Dear Name:

We regret that we can no longer extend credit to you due to your slow payment history. For all future orders we must require cash in advance or payment on delivery.

If you wish to reestablish credit at some future time, please contact our credit department at (123) 456-7890.

Sincerely,

Collection Letter

Situation   *Collection letters can be pleasant in tone. This letter is a friendly reminder that payment is due.*

The Letter   Dear Name:

I know how hectic our lives get and how easy it is to overlook little things. That is the reason I am sending you this reminder. Our records show your account has a balance due of $500.

Would you please take a few minutes to take care of this matter? If there are any problems, please let us know.

Thank you for your prompt attention.

Sincerely,

Collection Letter, 30-Day Reminder

Situation   *No one likes to chase after customers to remind them to pay their bills, but sadly, this is often necessary. Early reminders are courteous and assume that lack of payment is merely an oversight on the part of the customer.*

The Letter   Dear Name:

Our records show that payment for your December bill is late. The bustle of the end-of-year holidays often interrupts one's normal routine, so perhaps you forgot or even misplaced your last statement. That's why we're enclosing another one for your convenience.

Please accept this reminder that payment is now due. If your check is already on its way to us, disregard this notice.

Thank you for your cooperation.

Sincerely,

Collection Letter, 60-Day Reminder

Situation   *Second and third notices are shorter and more curt. These reminder letters point out that the customer's good account status is in jeopardy.*

The Letter   Dear Name:

Our records show that your account is now 60 days past due. A statement of outstanding invoices is attached for your records.

To keep your account in good standing, payment must be made immediately. If you have any questions or wish to make special arrangements for payment, please contact our accounts receivable department at (123) 456-7890.

Your attention to this matter will be greatly appreciated.

Sincerely,

Collection Letter, Over 90 Days

Situation   *Collection letters for long overdue accounts are forceful reminders that legal action will soon be taken. These notices are typically sent via Certified Mail or Return Receipt Requested.*

The Letter   Dear Name:

We still haven't heard from you regarding the outstanding balance owed on your account. A statement is enclosed.

To avoid having your account closed, please remit payment immediately. Failure to respond could result in damage to your credit rating and additional legal action.

We urge you to send us a check before March 15. If you wish to discuss special arrangements for payment, please contact us at (123) 456-7890.

Sincerely,

Collection Letter, Final Notice

Situation   *A final notice urges the customer one last time to pay what is owed. Here is a typical final notice to a delinquent customer.*

The Letter

Dear Name:

Your account is now in arrears $987.65. Copies of outstanding invoices are attached.

If we do not receive payment in full by September 7, your account will be closed and service will be canceled. In addition, this matter will be turned over to our collection agency.

Please call us within the next three business days to discuss how we can resolve this matter.

Sincerely,

Community Service—Invitation to Join a Board

Situation

This organization is inviting the recipient to join the board of directors of a civic organization. The letter sells the organization well, explaining how important its mission is.

The Letter

Dear Name:

We are all aware of the toll addiction can take on our community. Transitions House is a project organized to tackle the problem head-on.

With the help of city service agencies and law enforcement agencies and the cooperation of the judicial system, certain teenagers are offered a one-time opportunity to participate in this program. These young men and women are given intensive counseling, job training, and other skills needed to become productive citizens. Approximately 85 teenagers each year graduate from this two-year intensive program.

This year we have expanded our operations, and we need your help. We are inviting you to join our executive board of directors. The board consists of business professionals such as yourself, who can assist us in directing, organizing, and implementing the large fund-raising campaign that we must undertake soon. The executive board meets the first Tuesday of each month and select committees meet an additional one or two times a month.

Please join us. Transitions House and the teenagers who live there need you.

Sincerely,

Community Service—Volunteers Needed

Situation   *There are many ways for a company to support the community. Here, the business donates space and encourages employees to donate time.*

The Letter   We are proud to announce that we have made arrangements with City Community College to teach two courses on our premises after hours. These courses are English as a Second Language and Adult Literacy.

You can help by volunteering to be a tutor or teacher's aide in these classes. If you wish to donate your time, we will give you a stipend for your evening meal on the nights that you volunteer.

We feel that these programs are vital to business success and will also contribute to the community at large. For more information contact Mary Smith at extension 123.

Company Outing

Situation   *Company outings give employees a chance to socialize and get to know each other a little better.*

The Letter   Dear Name:

The annual company picnic will be held Saturday, July 5, at City Park starting at noon. We have reserved Pavilion C for our use. Employees, spouses, and children are invited. A delicious picnic lunch and soft drinks will be provided for everyone.

The softball game usually starts around 2 p.m. Bring chairs or blankets so you can be comfortable while you cheer your favorite players from the sidelines. There will also be balloons, face-painting, and a magician for the children.

We must remind you that the park prohibits alcoholic beverages. Please respect this ordinance.

Company Sports

Situation   *Many businesses sponsor company sports. The camaraderie among teammates often carries over into the workplace.*

The Letter   Bowling season is about to begin. Come one, come all. The only requirement is the desire to have fun.

Starting October 4, lanes are reserved at Panorama Bowl on Tuesday evenings from 7 p.m. to 9 p.m. The two best teams will represent our company at the Industrial League Playoffs. Last year, the Order Department team made the quarterfinals!

If you're interested in joining the company league, please call John Doe at extension 123.

Condo Maintenance Fee

Situation   *This form letter explains maintenance costs and serves as an invoice.*

The Letter   Dear Name:

The 19xx expenses for snow removal and grounds care are listed below. The snow removal costs were higher than normal because of February's winter storm. Expenses are shared among all tenants. Costs are prorated based upon square footage.

Snow removal, January - March 19xx	$1,200
Grounds care, 19xx	$4,030
Total	$5,230

Based on square footage of _____ , your cost is $_____.
Payment in full is due April 1. An envelope is enclosed for your convenience.

If you have any questions, call Jane Doe at 123-4567.

Sincerely,

Condo Association Board

Condolence Letter

Situation

No one's life is without loss, or even tragedy. When a loved one passes away, we often feel overwhelmed by loss and grief. Notes from friends and acquaintances are invaluable, for they help us feel less alone. As a friend, you may struggle with your words, wondering if you're saying the right thing. The surviving family members might not have met you, particularly if you are a business associate, so explain how you knew the deceased, and say what you will miss about that person. If you write simply and from your heart, your letter will bring comfort to the family.

The Letter

Dear Name:

I was saddened to learn that John Doe has passed away. He was a good friend to me at work, and he will be missed by his colleagues here.

I had the good fortune to work with John at XYZ for the last six years. He was a quiet mentor to me, willing to take the time to answer my questions and teach me more about our industry. He was always cheerful and pleasant, and his leadership was a great asset to our company.

Please accept my sincere condolences. May the sorrow of his passing soon be replaced by the peace and comfort of his memory.

With deepest sympathy,

Condolence Letter

Situation   *This employer is expressing sympathy by making a memorial donation in the name of the deceased. It is a meaningful gesture that will be appreciated.*

The Letter   Dear Name:

We are so sorry to learn of the death of your wife. She was a good friend to all of us here and we will miss her.

A contribution to the memorial fund at XZY Charity has been made in her name. You and your family are in our thoughts and prayers. Please accept our heartfelt condolences.

With deepest sympathy,

Confirm Agreement

Situation   *This letter confirms a discussion. The writer wants to confirm the agreement right away to prevent misunderstandings later.*

The Letter   Dear Name:

It was good talking to you this afternoon and sharing the news that I have been invited to be a guest on "Woodworking TV" show this summer. You have agreed to pick up any lodging, meal, and transportation expenses that I will incur when I tape this show.

This will be an opportunity to display my work and, of course, promote the book that you published. I will be in touch with you as soon as I receive more details from the producer.

Sincerely,

Confirm Appointment

Situation   *This letter confirms details of a telephone conversation. The writer specifies what documents will be brought to the next meeting. If additional documents will be needed, the recipient will know to clarify this.*

The Letter   Dear Name:

I appreciate your helpful telephone conversation today regarding setting up a trust fund for my mother.

As discussed, the trust you recommend will include both her monetary assets and her home. In addition, the trust can be used to pay her routine bills. It is my understanding that the bank will handle this for a small fee.

I will be with my mother at our meeting scheduled for January 19th at 10 a.m. I will bring a list of her assets, including bank accounts and insurance policies.

Thanks again for your help. My mother and I look forward to meeting with you.

Sincerely,

Confirm Appointment

Situation   *Confirming appointments saves time—time that would be wasted if you went to someone's place of business and that person was unable to see you after all. Although you could confirm the appointment with a phone call, the fact that you took the time to write a letter means this meeting is significant.*

The Letter   Dear Name:

It was good to talk to you this afternoon. As we discussed, I'll be at your office Thursday at 2 p.m. to finalize packaging designs. Mock-ups are being shipped for arrival tomorrow morning to give you an advance look.

Look forward to seeing you. By the way, if my office staff had a vote, the blue and orange version would win.

Sincerely,

Confirm Arrangements

Situation *A confirmation letter verifies information, usually details or decisions that were made quickly or orally. The letter can be brief, but it should cover all the details to make sure there were no misunderstandings. This letter is friendly and fun because the golfers have known each other for a long time. However, the reason for writing is to confirm the day's plans.*

The Letter Dear Name:

This letter will confirm our arrangements for the golf outing next Saturday.

Our foursome will include John and Jill along with you and me. We'll meet at the pro shop at 9:30 and pick up our carts there. Tee time is 10 a.m. sharp. After a rousing 18-hole game (which Jill thinks she'll win), we'll have a late lunch at the clubhouse.

My putting is still lousy, but if you spend your usual amount of time in the sand traps, it should be an even match.

Best regards,

Confirm Decisions

Situation

In a productive business meeting, many ideas are shared. As the project develops and plans become more focused, individuals agree to do additional work on various segments before they meet again. A memo confirming who is going to do what helps makes sure that the work will be completed on time. Any misunderstandings will be evident as soon as the memo is circulated.

The Letter

To: Names

From: John Doe

Re: Packaging Report

This will confirm our decisions of this morning's meeting.

1. Sam will rework the proposal on food service disposables.

2. Marjorie will continue her research on stretch and shrink film.

3. Bill and I will continue to investigate the problems we are having with our old packaging equipment and get costs on keeping this equipment operational for another 18 months.

Once we get these details in order, we should be ready to present our final report to the finance committee at their August meeting.

Regards,

Confirm Decisions

Situation   *An important reason for confirming what happened at a meeting is to remind participants of what they agreed to do. If the meeting was long and covered many different topics, they might forget.*

The Letter   Dear Name:

The first meeting of the Choral Parents Association (CPA) went quite well. Thanks for your enthusiastic remarks. Next Friday's concert will be a grand kickoff for the choral season.

Joan Delta and Doug Reilly will set up a table near the entrance to the auditorium to encourage parents to join the CPA. Parents who volunteered to help with refreshments are:

Bill and Sylvia Martinez—paper cups and napkins

Trent Brock—cookies

Sally Smith—apple cider

John and Lynn Baker—brownies

Look forward to seeing you at the concert.

Best regards,

Confirm Intent

Situation   *Sometimes the outcome of a meeting is simply to agree to continue working together. This letter confirms the intent of a recent meeting—that the relationship between the two companies is expected to be long and prosperous.*

The Letter   Dear Name:

Mary Smith and I certainly enjoyed meeting with you to discuss a possible partnering agreement between XYZ and QRS. Both Mary and I feel that our initial discussions were positive, but we want to put something in writing that signifies our intent.

As a start, I am writing up the notes of our meeting and Mary is drafting a broad letter indicating the plans XYZ has with regard to installing QRS systems in its four northern plants. As we all agreed, this should enhance the funding for working capital for QRS.

I think we are all pleased that this potential partnership is off to such a good start.

Sincerely,

Confirm Travel Arrangements

Situation

Travel arrangements should always be confirmed in writing because the people involved might not be able to contact each other once they have departed from home or office. The letter becomes a point of reference if the arrival is delayed.

The Letter

Dear Name:

Thanks for offering to pick me up at the airport next Wednesday. Wait for me in your car near baggage claim. I'll look for you there. My flight plans are:

Arrive Chicago 2:45 p.m., United Air Lines, Flight # 321

Like you, I'll be staying at the hotel that is adjacent to the conference center. Thanks in advance for the ride. It will be nice to see you and have a chance to catch up before the conference starts.

Warmest regards,

Confirm Verbal Discussion

Situation   *Confirming a verbal agreement is a good idea. In fact, had this writer confirmed the first discussion, the misunderstanding would have come to light right away.*

The Letter   Dear Name:

I am sending under separate cover a check for $7,879.00 for the fall semester at State University. As discussed, you have reinstated Mary Smith for the fall semester and her original schedule has not changed.

To recap my experience, I never received an invoice for the tuition. Last week I called and requested a duplicate invoice which Mr. John Doe told me would be mailed that day. He also said that in any event the cut-off date for the fall semester was August 12— which he would extend to August 21. Imagine my surprise this morning when I learned that the deadline for Mary's tuition payment had passed.

Thank you for your help in this matter. The check will be in your hands before noon tomorrow via overnight mail delivery. Note that this is within the original deadline I was given over the telephone last week by Mr. Doe.

Sincerely,

Confirmation to Speaker

Situation   *Guest speakers are often hired during a phone call, but the booking is not really set until it is in writing. If you do not confirm the booking within a reasonable amount of time, the speaker is liable to assume you have changed your mind and thus accept a different booking on that date.*

The Letter   Dear Name:

We are delighted that you will be presenting your seminar, "Instilling Workplace Teamwork," at our company next January. I am enclosing two copies of our contract. For your convenience a mailer and label are also enclosed.

Would you please return the following:

- several slides to help us promote your training sessions

- a supply list for workshop participants

- one signed contract (The second copy is for your file.)

You may want to make your flight reservations now so that you can take advantage of bargain air fares. Our training director will meet you at the airport and make arrangements for meals and hotel accommodations for the week that you are teaching.

Sincerely,

Congratulations Letter

Situation

Business is not necessarily easy—it's called "work" for good reason—and successes are often hard won. The success might be a promotion, an industry award, or community recognition. Take time to write a quick letter acknowledging another's success. That person will remember you kindly for it.

The Letter

Dear Name:

Congratulations! I was delighted to see in *Industry Times* that you are now division manager supervising small-cap stock holdings at American Federal Trust. AmFed is fortunate to have you on their team, and I want to wish you great success in your new position.

Sincerely,

Congratulations on Promotion

Situation   *Be sure to congratulate another on a promotion. Even if you are a bit miffed, your letter is a nice way to show that you will cooperate nonetheless. This writer is genuinely pleased at the other's success.*

The Letter   Dear Name:

Congratulations on your new position as vice president. This is a well-earned promotion indeed. Under your direction, this division has grown to become one of the largest in the company. I am confident your ideas, inspiration, and leadership will make us an industry leader.

Please accept my very best wishes for continued success.

Sincerely,

Contract Cover Letter

Situation   *Short letters are fine. This letter is a simple transmittal, but the writer takes advantage of the opportunity to reinforce a positive working relationship.*

The Letter   Dear Name:

Enclosed is your copy of the signed contract. I am confident this signals the beginning of a long and prosperous relationship between our companies.

Thanks for your help in these negotiations. I'm pleased, as I'm sure you are, with the positive results.

Sincerely,

Contract Cover Letter

Situation   *This letter accompanies a contract. The writer also uses the letter to assure the recipients that they made a good decision.*

The Letter   Dear Name:

I am enclosing the listing contract on your home. The duration of the contract is 90 days; the commission and list price are as we agreed. Please return it right away so that I can enter the information in the computer network. A self-addressed, stamped envelope is enclosed for your convenience in returning the signed contract.

I took some color pictures of the house and lot today. As soon as the snow melts, I will take new pictures to feature the lake and green grass.

Our agency is the largest in this area, and we do more advertising than any other agency, week in and week out. I am confident you'll be pleased with our service.

Sincerely,

Contract Cover Letter

Situation   *This letter accompanies a signed contract and refers to a future venture that has been arranged.*

The Letter   Dear Name:

Enclosed are three copies of our most recent agreement. The original is archived in our files. I speak for all of us here when I say we are looking forward to a long and prosperous business relationship.

Everyone in your organization has been a pleasure to work with, and we look forward to sharing our booth with your marketing team at the next vendor show.

Sincerely,

Contract Enclosed

Situation   *A transmittal letter is a good idea if a contract is being sent. You can remind the recipient of any special instructions and use the transmittal letter to express goodwill.*

The Letter   Dear Roy:

I am pleased to enclose two copies of the contract for the proposed manufacturing facility.

Please sign and date both copies. Your signature should be witnessed—someone in your office can do this, signing to the left of your signature. Return one signed copy to me.

This new venture promises to be an excellent employment opportunity, and this facility will help the county attract more corporations to the area. Congratulations on your hard work, too. Thanks to your persistence and ability to coordinate all parties concerned, we are progressing nicely.

Sincerely,

Contract Enclosed

Situation   *In this example, changes to an existing contract have to be initialed by all parties, but it is a formality at this point. The writer is also using the transmittal letter to remind the recipient of an important meeting.*

The Letter   Dear Name:

The changes we agreed upon are inserted in the enclosed contracts. Bob Jones, our division manager, initialed the changes and signed both copies. Please add your initials to each change, then return one copy to me.

John Doe, chief engineer for XYZ Construction, will have updated plans for the drainage tiles ready by Thursday. I'd like for you to meet with John and me Friday at 10 a.m. to go over the revisions. Mary Smith will be there, too; she wants to be sure the county's environmental concerns have been addressed satisfactorily.

By the way, we're still on schedule for an August opening.

Best regards,

Contract Negotiations

Situation   *This internal memo describes a current situation and suggests that the customer's point of view has merit.*

The Letter   Dear Name:

Attached is a letter from XYZ Company. They want to do business with us but feel our contract is too restrictive and is much more adversarial than our competitors' contracts. Frankly, I think XYZ has a point. However, my concern is not only with XYZ but also whether we are turning away future suppliers.

Our current supplier is QRS Corp. Their products are overpriced, their service is lousy, and the products in question aren't selling. XYZ can give us the same product, better service, and a much better price.

Our contract people are working with XYZ to come up with a contract that both parties can live with and I think that we will be able to succeed in this. However, the original problem remains, i.e., our current contract is too rigid and inflexible.

Let's meet to discuss how we might address this issue.

Sincerely,

Contract Negotiations

Situation   *Contract negotiations can be difficult. Here, the writer is making an important point—that the company is not going to write a special contract for this customer.*

The Letter   Dear Name:

Thank you for your fax today. I appreciate your concern and am sorry you are so dissatisfied with our contract. I suggest that we negotiate in good faith, remembering that our business relationship is a profitable one for both of us.

Although our legal department is willing to make some modifications within reason, they are not ready to rewrite the entire contract. That being said, what changes are acceptable to both of us? Let's start with Articles D and J and go from there.

I'll be in the office until 2 p.m. today and expect to be available the rest of the week. I look forward to further discussions with you.

Sincerely,

Contract Negotiations

Situation   *This letter indicates that negotiations have been friendly and that both sides have worked to find a mutually acceptable contract.*

The Letter   Dear Name:

This is to follow up on the voice mail I left yesterday. Thanks for your patience while we have been studying your proposal. Your last letter clarified the issues quite well.

Attached are our suggestions for the five sections that are being modified. I am pleased that we are close to language that both of us can live with, and I hope you will agree that we are quite close to finalizing this deal.

As soon as you give me your okay, I'll have the contracts drawn up and ready for signatures. Thanks again for your help and cooperation.

Sincerely,

Contract Renewal

Situation   *Many companies support local service organizations by advertising in their promotional booklets. This organization is asking that the advertiser renew for the coming year.*

The Letter   Dear Name:

Enclosed is an advertiser form and a copy of your ad from last year.

You can once again help us continue to serve those who are recovering from substance abuse simply by placing an ad in our annual ad book. This soft-covered book is given away at our January banquet and mailed with our calendar throughout the year. For a very nominal fee your ad will reach over 5,000 customers. In addition, we acknowledge your support in each of our quarterly newsletters.

Please complete the attached form, making any changes to last year's ad, then send it back to me. Enclose payment now, or fax your ad and we'll invoice you later.

Thanks again for your continuing support of this organization.

Sincerely,

Convention Request

Situation   *It costs money to send employees to trade shows. This writer wants to attend a particular convention and writes to a superior, justifying and selling the idea.*

The Letter   Dear Name:

I would like your permission to attend the national industry convention in Houston. Because this show is held only every other year, I think we are missing an important opportunity if we don't attend. This show serves the plastics industry, which for us is a very large market. There are 450 vendors expected this year, and several of our competitors will be exhibiting.

I feel I am the most qualified member of the team to attend. My three largest accounts will be exhibiting, and I will be able to scout for new products and trends. I will also have the opportunity to meet with many of my other customers.

A budget for travel and other related expenses is attached. Give me a call if you have any questions.

Sincerely,

Correction Request

Situation   *When inaccurate information is published about a person or business, the mere fact that the information appeared in print tends to give it credibility.*

The Letter   Dear Name:

It has come to my attention that some of my biographical information is incorrect in your book, *Important People*.

1. *Birth name Mary Doe.* Doe is my mother's maiden name. My birth name is Mary Smith; I continue to use it.

2. *Born to European immigrants.* I was born to American citizens who were themselves children of American citizens. Family records indicate that my ancestors immigrated from Australia in the 1850s.

While these errors may appear relatively inconsequential, they do perpetuate incorrect information about me. Please correct this information in your next edition. I would appreciate acknowledgment and confirmation at your earliest convenience.

Sincerely,

Correction Request

Situation   *This letter points out an apparent error. The writer asks for an explanation or correction.*

The Letter   Dear Name:

I have your invoice 1234 dated June 22, but there seems to be a discrepancy. The replication charge on your pricing sheet is 85 cents per 1000, but on the invoice it is $1.25 per 1000.

We need to clear this up before I can process your invoice for payment. If this is an input error, just send a corrected statement to my attention.

Sincerely,

CPR Classes

Situation

This business is offering CPR classes to employees. Classes are held on company premises to make it easy for all employees to learn this lifesaving technique.

The Letter

We are pleased to offer free CPR classes to all employees. The cardiopulmonary resuscitation technique is easy to learn and has saved many lives.

Emergency Medical Technicians from the Fire Department will be teaching the class. Instruction includes a film, a booklet, and the chance to practice on a special CPR dummy.

We encourage all employees to sign up for the classes. CPR training takes only one morning a year. Be prepared for an emergency. Call John Doe at Ext. 123 to reserve a seat for yourself.

Customer Complaint

Situation   *This complaint letter is from a customer who was disappointed that an expected service was not available.*

The Letter   Dear Name:

I am writing to express my extreme disappointment. I recently discovered that your restaurant does not offer valet parking as advertised.

I went to your restaurant Wednesday night, but there was no valet parking and there were no empty spaces in your parking lot, so I had to park in the public parking lot across the street. Because there is no traffic light at the corner, I had some difficulty crossing the busy four-lane street in front of your restaurant. Getting to and from my car for dinner was dangerous and unsettling.

I think you should stop advertising valet parking when obviously it is not always available.

Sincerely,

Customer Request

Situation *This type of request is very common. Many customers will make a phone call rather than write a letter. In either case, a courteous reply is required.*

The Letter Dear Name:

After reading about your product in this month's issue of *Industry News*, I would like to receive more information.

Please send me the name of a local source where I can examine this product and perhaps see it in use.

Thank you.

Sincerely,

Deadline Approaching

Situation   *Distributors' catalogs are important sales tools, and suppliers benefit by having their products included. In this case, the supplier has been tardy in forwarding information, and a final print deadline is fast approaching.*

The Letter   Dear Name:

This is a reminder that we still need some information from you in order to include your product line in our spring catalog. The two items still outstanding are:

1. *Wholesale price information*—We will run a price merge against your disk to generate the retail prices that will appear in the catalog.

2. *Negatives*—We need color-separated negatives for the seven products listed. The black/white scans you sent are suitable for page layout position only; the quality is inadequate for the final printing.

The deadline for receiving this material is January 7. Please note that this is an absolute deadline. If we do not have the material in our hands by 5 p.m., the three pages devoted to your products will be taken out of the catalog.

If there is anything we can do here to assist you, please let me know.

Sincerely,

Decline Appointed Position

Situation   *It is an honor to be asked to help run a civic organization. This writer declines, but offers words of support to the organization.*

The Letter   Dear Name:

I am honored by your invitation to join the board of directors of the Civic Disaster Relief Committee. For several years I have volunteered my time for fund-raising efforts by this committee and I fully support your work.

However, due to other professional commitments at this time, I must regretfully decline your invitation. Although I will continue to volunteer my services for occasional events, I feel that I am unable to contribute the time that this position would require.

Thank you again for thinking of me.

Sincerely,

Decline Corporate Donation

Situation

It is always more difficult to say no than yes. This brief letter is cordial, but the business declines to participate.

The Letter

Dear Name:

You are certainly to be commended for the work that Safehouse Charities is doing. We thank you for the invitation to be a corporate sponsor, but our company policy prevents us from participating.

We wish your organization much success in its endeavors.

Sincerely,

Decline Invitation

Situation   *Businesspeople use trade shows and industry conferences to network. In this instance, the writer is unable to attend, but wishes to make contact soon afterward.*

The Letter   Dear Name:

Thank you for the invitation to be your guest at the information systems conference next month. Unfortunately, business commitments on the West Coast will make it impossible for me to attend. I appreciate your thoughtfulness and hope that I will be able to attend next year.

I will give you a call when I return from Los Angeles so we can set up a lunch date.

Best regards,

Decline Invitation to Speak

Situation   *If you are invited to make a presentation to an organization but must decline, you might want to suggest another qualified speaker. You will be helping out both the program person and the second speaker, and they will remember you for it.*

The Letter   Dear Name:

I am very sorry that I will be unable to accept your invitation to speak at the Lewis Quilting Guild on Wednesday, October 17th.

If you do not have another speaker in mind, I can highly recommend Mary Smith. Mary is a noted authority on the care and conservation of antique quilts and is highly regarded as a speaker. Her lecture generally includes a slide show, and she also teaches workshops. You can reach her at (123) 456-7890.

Thank you again for your kind invitation. I hope I will be able to meet with your guild at another time.

Sincerely,

Decline Membership

Situation   *This writer declines an invitation to help oversee and manage a volunteer organization. Note that a detailed explanation is unnecessary. The letter is brief, but gracious.*

The Letter   Dear Name:

Thank you for your letter of July 14 inviting me to join the executive board of your fine organization. Unfortunately, I must decline because of other personal and professional commitments.

I would like to commend your organization for the important contribution it makes to our community, and I wish you and the other board members continued success.

Very truly yours,

Decline Social Invitation

Situation   *This short letter declines a social invitation. The writer also extends good wishes for the happy occasion*

The Letter

Dear Name:

Thanks for the inviting us to your anniversary party, but unfortunately we will be unable to attend.

Please accept our congratulations and best wishes for continued happiness.

Best wishes,

Decline Use of Name

Situation   *If you do not wish to allow your name to be used by a charitable organization, you need only say no. You can decline graciously, yet perhaps choose to support the organization's efforts in a more quiet way.*

The Letter   Dear Name:

I am complimented by your request to use my name as a sponsor for Safehouse Charities. Although I certainly support and applaud the good work that Safehouse Charities has accomplished in our community, it is my policy not to lend my name to fundraising efforts.

A contribution is enclosed as support for your efforts. However, your records must show this as an anonymous donation.

Good luck with this year's fund-raising efforts. Keep up your important work.

Sincerely,

Delayed Shipment

Situation   *Shipments are delayed for many reasons, including missing authorization from the customer. Here the writer gently prods the customer, pointing out that only the customer can move things along.*

The Letter   Dear Name:

Your shipment of glass beakers has been delayed because we still have not received written authorization from you.

The easiest solution might be to send us a purchase order. You can simply fax it to the above number. As soon as we hear from you, we can notify our shipping department to release your order.

Sincerely,

Deny Credit

Situation   *A customer who might not pay is a poor customer indeed. This letter states that once a positive record of payment is established, the business will consider changing a customer's account status from cash to credit.*

The Letter   Dear Name:

We regret that at this time we cannot extend an open account status to your company because we are unable to establish a record of payment history.

We will, however, be happy to do business with you on a cash basis at the present time. As our relationship continues, we will be more than willing to reevaluate this situation.

Thank you for your interest. We look forward to your first order.

Sincerely,

Deny Customer Request

Situation

This letter is denying the customer's request, but in a most positive manner. The writer explains that the customer has sufficient user information for the machine purchased, then offers a discount that the customer can use toward a future purchase.

The Letter

Dear Name:

Your request for a complete operations manual for the Model 123 machine was recently forwarded to my attention.

The model you ordered (123) is shipped with the abridged operations booklet and Quick Reference card. The 123 booklet covers all the features available on this model. You indicated that you already have this information.

The complete operations manual is included with Model 99. This is our top-of-the line machine and many features are available on this model only. I am enclosing a discount certificate for you to use on your next order with us. You can also apply this to a Model 99 upgrade.

I hope this answers your questions. We look forward to doing business with you again soon.

Sincerely,

Distributor Request

This letter deserves attention because it indicates the writer is seriously interested.

The Letter

Dear Name:

I am interested in becoming a distributor of your product. I market related supplies to retail customers and your product would be a good addition to my inventory.

I am interested in minimum orders, quantity discounts, and a suggested pricing structure. Please let me know what you require in order to become a distributor.

Sincerely,

Donation Request

Situation   *This charitable organization is asking local businesses to donate money, goods, or services. Many businesses will contribute, recognizing that it is good business to invest in the local community.*

The Letter   Dear Name:

XYZ Services is a social service agency in this county serving the needs of families at risk. XYZ Services recently purchased a building but it needs major repairs and renovations to comply with city building codes. The counseling office also needs office furniture and equipment, especially a photocopier.

Your company can help XYZ Services by providing funds in the form of a grant or by donating goods and services. A copy of XYZ's tax exempt certificate is attached.

Thank you in advance for your support.

Sincerely,

Employee Wellness Report

Situation   *This letter reports on the benefits of supporting an employee wellness program.*

The Letter   Dear Name:

At your request, I've been investigating the possibility of setting up a corporate membership plan for our employees at the XYZ Health Club.

The club has state-of-the-art equipment and a superb facility. It has more to offer than most because it is affiliated with QRS hospital. For example, most of their fitness specialists have a degree in this field; the rest are at least certified in their specialty. They also bring in hospital personnel, such as physical therapists and dieticians, for special programs.

If our company participates, employees will receive 50% off the enrollment fee plus a free fitness profile once a year. The company will receive a monthly utilization report on the number of employee members and the frequency of use.

If we can encourage enough employees to use this facility on a regular basis, we will qualify for better rates on our group insurance policy. Regular exercise means better productivity, lower absentee rates, and better all-around health for employees.

A detailed proposal is attached. After you've had a chance to study this, let's get together to discuss it.

Best regards,

Error Investigation

Situation   *This letter goes to some length to reassure the customer that this atypical error was investigated and corrected.*

The Letter   Dear Name:

It was good to talk to you this morning and review the unusual situation with this customer. To recap, we inadvertently over-charged this customer due to an input error on our part. It raised the question of whether we might be violating our distribution agreement with you.

Our strategy is to honor your list price. We have not raised our selling price nor do we have any intention of interfering with your pricing strategies. Our policy is to avoid aggressive discounts. We feel our customers are buying extra services from us, including technical support and a very liberal return and warranty policy.

While we can't promise to never make mistakes, we can promise to fix them when they happen, as we did in this case. We value our partnership with you and look forward to a continued pleas-ant and profitable business relationship.

Sincerely,

Extend Credit to Cash Customer

Situation   *Once cash customers establish a track record of paying their bills in full and on time, many businesses extend offers for credit accounts.*

The Letter   Dear Name:

We would like to thank you for your business for the past two years.

To show our appreciation of your excellent payment history, we can now open a credit account for your company. Our terms are 2/10 net 30.

We value your business and look forward to a long and mutually profitable relationship.

Sincerely,

Fact-Finding Report

Situation   *This is a report for upper management. The writer reviews background information first, then describes the current status.*

The Letter   Dear Name:

We advertised a new electronic dispensing system in a promotional piece two years ago and sold approximately 100 units. Because of problems with our supplier, however, we ultimately discontinued the product. XYZ Company is able to make a small dispensing system similar to the original one, and we can label it with our in-house trademark. I should have a prototype in the coming weeks. At that time, I'll ask our engineering group to test this unit to ensure it is a quality product for our customers.

Note that this dispensing system is similar to the version we sell to manufacturing plants; in fact this model uses the same casing. Attached is a detailed description of how it can be customized for our retail customers along with a cost comparison of competing units.

John Doe is looking into the trademark application and expects to have information by the end of next week.

Sincerely,

Final Settlement

Situation   *Because of previous legal action, the writer is asking the recipient to sign a statement agreeing that the bill has been paid in full and the matter is settled. In these situations, it is always advisable to have your attorney or legal department draft the letter for you.*

The Letter   Dear Name:

Enclosed is a check in the amount of $1,234.56 as full and final payment for obligations of XYZ Company. This check is in reference to the small claims action brought by QRS against XYZ in March of 19XX.

By accepting this check for this amount, you release XYZ Company from all obligations in connection with this matter. Please show your agreement by countersigning in the space provided below.

Thank you for your consideration in this matter.

Sincerely,

Accepted this ___ day of _____, 19____

By _____.

Financial Negotiations

Situation

Financial compromises are part of business. Before negotiating, however, make sure the terms are in keeping with company policy. In this case, the writer is asking for management approval before going back to the customer.

The Letter

Dear Name:

The billing discrepancy between us and supplier XYZ seems to have reached an impasse. XYZ claims that we owe $14,000 for merchandise that was drop-shipped to various stores across the country. Our records, however, show that we only received $8,700 worth of merchandise.

To resolve this situation, my suggestion is that we split the difference and offer them $2,650, which is half of the $5,300 discrepancy.

May I have your approval to go ahead with this? I would like to get this matter settled by the end of the fiscal quarter.

Regards,

Financial Settlement

Situation   *This is a good example of a memo that might be written by a comptroller to an accounting manager. The response here is probably not what the manager expected.*

The Letter   Dear Name:

Thank you for your memo of November 6th updating me on the billing discrepancy between us and supplier XYZ in the amount of $9,000.

Rather than split the difference, I feel we should pay the full amount in order to maintain a good relationship. XYZ's products sell well and we have no history of problems with them.

Remember to show this adjustment on the inventory records.

Regards,

Follow-Up for Goodwill

Situation

Some meetings need only a brief written follow-up. In this case, the recipient did not participate in the major part of the meeting, but is still involved in the project. The letter is a friendly status report.

The Letter

Dear Name:

It was great seeing you again, and I was pleased that you could drop by to say hello to everyone.

As you know, the problems with Allied Construction have been resolved and the stone masonry fireplace project is moving along on schedule. As soon as the building site pictures are developed, I will send you a set. Now that we have a green light and the project is back on track, it should be completed by the end of June.

Thanks too for recommending the latest industry tell-all book. I picked up a copy in the airport and started reading it on the plane home last night. Very revealing—am surprised that this information didn't surface much earlier.

Best regards,

Follow-Up Report to Customer

Situation   *Even though a project is ongoing, you might want to write a brief note so your customer knows you're following through with the items you discussed.*

The Letter   Dear Name:

I just wanted to thank you for taking the time to meet and talk with me when I was in Atlanta two weeks ago. I am enclosing some possible brochure ideas that came to mind after our discussion. I hope these are on the right track; give me a call and let me know what you think.

One of our copywriters is putting together some ideas for the advertising series you mentioned in our last phone call. I hope to have something more for you next week. Meanwhile, thanks again for your time and courtesy.

Cordially,

Free Offer

Situation

Business freebies are designed to get the customer in the door. In this instance, the customer has to listen to a sales pitch and try out the product before getting the "free" book.

The Letter

Dear Name:

The next time you take a test drive, I would like you to have the latest edition of *Tourist Attraction Travel Guide* with my compliments. This guide contains a list of the best motels, hotels, and bed and breakfast inns throughout the continental United States. It also includes tourist attractions that are popular in each state.

To see the country, of course, you'll want to travel in style, comfort, and safety. So come to XYZ Auto and choose the car, truck, or van that will make your vacation perfect. We have the latest models in stock, and every one can be custom ordered to your specifications.

Our showroom is open every day from 9 a.m. to 9 p.m. When you stop by, our salespeople will be happy to let you take a test drive in your dream car. Then the travel guide will be yours.

Sincerely,

Freelance Agreement

Situation   *This letter confirms the agreement between the freelance employee and the company. Many companies have special contracts for their freelance employees.*

The Letter   Dear Name:

This will confirm our conversation of this morning. Even though you have retired from this company, you are willing to continue working as a freelance contractor on the XYZ project. This project is expected to last six months.

We are pleased that you are willing to help us see this project through to its completion. I look forward to seeing you again Monday morning. Please stop by Human Resources first to complete the necessary paperwork.

Best regards,

Get Well Thoughts

Situation

When a friend is suffering from a serious illness, you might want to do something more than send a get-well card. A short personal note will let your friend know that you care.

The Letter

Dear Name:

I just learned of your illness and wanted you to know that I am thinking of you. I hope your treatments are progressing without complications and you will soon be up and around.

When you feel stronger, give me a call. I'd love to have you join me for lunch. Meanwhile, best wishes for a speedy recovery.

Sincerely,

Holiday Greetings

Situation   *Many businesses send holiday greetings to their customers. Some businesses include special holiday offers, but this one merely says thank you to customers. Notice that there are no references to specific religions.*

The Letter   Dear Name:

XYZ Corporation would like to extend our very best wishes for this holiday season. We appreciate your past business and look forward to serving you in the future.

May the coming year bring peace and prosperity to you and yours.

Sincerely,

Informal Agreement

Situation   *You don't necessarily need a lawyer for every business deal. If the parties trust each other and have already agreed, the terms can be stated in a brief letter. By writing the letter, you clarify what the job is, formalize the project, and prevent future misunderstandings.*

The Letter   Dear Name:

How nice it was to hear from you yesterday, and I am delighted to have the opportunity to work on your newest training manuals.

For the record, I suggest we do as before: I will rewrite your training manuals per your directions. My fee is $X/per hour, although we can easily change to a flat fee for the project at a later date. The only other charges will be standard office expenses such as phone, photo-copying, overnight shipping, and postage charges. Either of us can change these terms, including canceling, via fax, e-mail, or a phone call. I understand and accept that this is a rush project.

I look forward to having your first shipment of materials on my desk by the end of the week. It is a pleasure to be working with you once again.

Best personal regards,

Informal Invitation

Situation

Most social occasions are informal, but even informal ones deserve a written invitation. If the occasion implies a present—an anniversary or birthday party, for example—most guests will feel obligated to bring or send one unless you state otherwise.

The Letter

Dear Friends,

Please join us on September 12th to help celebrate our twenty-fifth wedding anniversary. We're having a garden party at home and would like you to join us for dinner and an evening of music and dancing, beginning at 7 p.m.

No gifts, please. It is enough that we have the fellowship and camaraderie of good friends to share our happiness.

Sincerely,

Information Needed

Situation   *Businesspeople read trade journals to keep abreast of industry trends and what other companies are doing. In this case, the writer learned more from an advertisement than from editorial copy.*

The Letter   Dear Name:

I opened the latest issue of *Industry Journal* magazine last night and was surprised to see XYZ's ad on page 14. I assume this means that XYZ, our biggest competitor, is introducing a new marketing program.

Please track this down and find out what is going on. I want to know if this is a regional test or a national campaign. Get back to me right away.

Thanks,

Introduce Opportunity

Situation   *This letter is sent to a list of potential clients. The writer hopes to spark the reader's interest and will probably follow up with additional mailings and phone calls.*

The Letter   Dear Name:

I am writing to introduce you to the potential of investment property here in Deerpath County. Right now Deerpath is the fastest growing county in the state. Many parcels of land are still available at realistic prices, and the interest rates are very favorable at this time.

Typical land parcels available include:

- 4+ acre site with frontage on Route 123.

- 5+ acre site on the corner of Routes 45 and 67.

- 9-acre parcel on Route 89 with great potential for an office building or small shopping center.

- Larger parcels from 40 acres to 180 acres are also available. Most of these parcels are rental farm acreage with a house and outbuildings on the property.

I've enclosed detailed listing sheets on each of the above parcels. As this area continues its growth and development, I invite you to let me show you what is available for your potential investment.

Sincerely,

Investigating Customer Complaint

Situation
The wise businessperson investigates all complaints carefully. If the fault is with the product, then more complaints are bound to follow. The goal of the investigation is to prevent problems, not assign blame.

The Letter
Dear Name:

Please take a look at the enclosed shirt. As you can see, it is covered with spots. The customer claims these spots appeared after washing the shirt in our detergent.

The sales representative has already interviewed the customer and found no unusual washing techniques that would harm the fabric. She did note that the shirt is made from Estersilk, XYZ's newest synthetic fiber.

Have your lab team run whatever tests are necessary to get to the bottom of this. The customer has already been reimbursed for the shirt, so you are free to cut the shirt into whatever pieces you need.

I would like a report on this within the next two weeks.

Thanks,

Investigation Report

Situation *This memo is reporting on a customer's claim. The writer has investigated the matter and is making a recommendation. The recipient will make the final decision on what to do.*

The Letter Dear Name:

I have been investigating XYZ's claim that merchandise was shipped to our Bradford branch, but the invoice was not paid. I feel this claim is questionable because there are no records at either the corporate office or the Bradford branch to show that merchandise was ever received.

In view of our history with this supplier—a history fraught with problems—I think a settlement on this disputed amount would be inappropriate. My recommendation is that we stand by our records. By offering to settle dubious claims such as this one, we may be sending the wrong signals to our other suppliers.

Sincerely,

Invitation for Interview

Situation   *This letter asks the recipient to come in for a personal interview.*

The Letter   Dear Name:

Thank you for your resume and recent letter expressing an interest in the available position.

We would like to meet with you and discuss your credentials and experience in greater detail. Please call my assistant, John Doe, to set up a convenient time.

We look forward to speaking with you further.

Sincerely,

Invitation to Try New Product

Situation *There are several ways to test-market a new product. Here, the developer invites possible buyers to see a demo and try it out.*

The Letter Dear Name:

You are cordially invited to a demonstration of our new software package Tuesday at 10:30 a.m. We would like you to participate in evaluating this software because we need your input.

We will be giving an overview of the capabilities and functions of the complete system package. The demonstration includes hands-on time for all participants. The system will be set up in our main office, conference room 3. Lunch will be served immediately afterward.

We appreciate your participation and look forward to your input.

Sincerely,

Invoice Error

Situation   *When pointing out a billing error, be sure to include all pertinent data. Your goal is to make it easy for the error to be corrected.*

The Letter   Dear Name:

Your invoice #1234 dated January 3rd contains an error. The shipment of precision machine tools was for four bench lathes and two grinders. We were billed for a third grinder which was not shipped.

I spoke to Mr. Anderson about this matter and he assured me that the extra charge would be removed from our invoice. However, as your statement shows, this has not yet happened. Please remove the $236.00 charge from this invoice and issue a corrected statement.

As soon as your revised statement arrives, I will see that payment is remitted.

Yours truly,

Job Inquiry

Situation

After doing business in one industry for a time, you are bound to develop a network of friends and associates. This network can be extremely helpful, as this letter shows.

The Letter

Dear Name:

My position with XYZ Company was recently eliminated due to restructuring within the company. As a result, I am seeking a new opportunity and hope to stay in the construction field.

I am hoping my broad-based sales and general management experience and network of contacts in the industry, including yourself, will help me uncover a position where I can significantly contribute to growth and profitability, as I did at XYZ.

I would appreciate any consideration you can give me should you know of anyone looking for an experienced leader.

Sincerely,

Job Inquiry

Situation   *This writer is asking if special credentials are required to work with this professional organization. At the same time, the writer's own qualifications are presented.*

The Letter   Dear Name:

I am interested in finding out more about presenting seminars to your organization. I have more than twenty years' experience in marketing products in this industry as well as seven years in sales, sales management, and advertising research. Specifics are outlined on the attached resume.

Please send me information on the requirements for being certified as an instructor for your association. Thank you for your help on this matter.

Sincerely,

Job Offer

Situation   *This offer of employment includes the job title and annual salary. Many businesses also state that employment is contingent on passing a drug test and verifying information on the application form. Because of the legal ramifications, letters like this one should be approved by an attorney or legal department to make sure they are in compliance with company policy and current hiring practices.*

The Letter   Dear Name:

We are pleased to offer you employment at XYZ company. We feel that your skills and background will be a valuable asset to our team.

Per our discussion, the position is Contracts Administrator in our Legal Department. Your immediate supervisor will be Mary Smith, Department Manager. Your starting date will be Monday, May 3. The starting salary is $28,000 per year and is paid on a bi-weekly basis. The enclosed Employee Handbook outlines the medical and retirement benefits that our company offers.

If you choose to accept this offer, please sign the second copy of this letter in the space provided and return it to us. A stamped, self-addressed envelope is enclosed for your convenience.

We look forward to welcoming you as a new employee at XYZ Corporation.

Sincerely,

Job Rejection

Situation

This letter states that there is no opening that matches the applicant's qualifications. The company will keep the application in an active file for six months.

The Letter

Dear Name:

Thank you for your recent letter and resume expressing your interest in working for XYZ company.

Unfortunately, we cannot be very encouraging at this time because we have no openings in your area of interest and expertise. However, we will keep your resume on file for six months in case such an opportunity opens up.

Thank you again for your interest in XYZ.

Sincerely,

Job Rejection

Situation   *An interview is an important step toward being hired, but it is not a guarantee either. This candidate was rejected after being interviewed.*

The Letter   Dear Name:

Thank you for coming to speak with us regarding the available position. We enjoyed having the opportunity to meet you and discuss your credentials.

While we were most impressed, we have identified another candidate whose background and experience better meet the requirements for this job.

Thank you again for your interest in XYZ Company. We wish you success in your job search.

Sincerely,

Job Termination

Situation   *There are many legitimate reasons for getting fired. This letter documents one such reason—not showing up for work.*

The Letter   Dear Name:

This is to notify you that your employment with our company is terminated as of today. The reason for your termination is job abandonment.

You have not been at work for five days nor have you made any effort to offer a satisfactory explanation for your absence.

The enclosed check is for wages earned up to the date of your termination.

Sincerely,

Job Termination

Situation   *Most businesses check the information on an application form very carefully. In this case, deception was uncovered after the employee had started working. Falsifying information makes a value statement about you. If you're willing to lie on an application, you may be willing to lie about many things.*

The Letter   Dear Name:

This letter will confirm our discussion. Your employment with this company is terminated, effective today, because of falsified information on your employee application.

Unfortunately, your action in this matter leaves us no choice. Our application form clearly states that falsifying information will lead to disciplinary action, up to and including dismissal.

Sincerely,

Job Warning

Situation   *This is a warning letter to an employee stating that abusing company privileges can lead to dismissal.*

The Letter   Dear Name:

This letter is to confirm our discussion of earlier today. Our company policy states that company credit cards are to be used for company business only. These cards are not authorized for personal use.

Using a company credit card again for your personal purchases will lead to disciplinary action, up to and including suspension of credit card privileges and termination of employment. All billing statements for company credit cards are scrutinized carefully. No one individual is singled out.

Please remember that it is a privilege to have the use of a company credit card. Treat this privilege with respect.

Sincerely,

Letter of Appreciation

Situation   *Everyone appreciates a letter that recognizes hard work and good success, particularly if it is sent by one's supervisor or manager.*

The Letter   Dear Name:

I just received the final sales numbers for the last fiscal year. Your sales increased more than 21%! This is simply outstanding, and I trust you too are pleased with the results.

My sincere thanks to your sales team for a great year. Congratulations!

Warm regards,

Letter to Ex-Customer

Situation   *This letter to an ex-customer asks why a competitor was chosen. If the customer answers (many won't), the business will learn something valuable about itself. It can take steps to correct any problems, decide to offer new products or extend additional services, and eventually try to win the customer back.*

The Letter   Dear Name:

It has been a privilege doing business with you these last years. I value your business and regret losing it.

It would be helpful if you would take a few minutes to let us know how you felt about our service and the reasons you decided to select another vendor. You can use the reverse side of this letter for any comments you want to make, or if it is easier, just give me a call. I will appreciate your candor and will hold your comments in strictest confidence.

I hope that in the future I will once again have the privilege of working with you.

Sincerely,

Meeting Materials

Situation   *Although this letter is confirming who will be at the meeting, the writer is also asking the recipient to follow up on two items in advance.*

The Letter   Dear Name:

Attached is a list of attendees who have accepted our invitation to the hardware demo next Thursday.

All of the vendors on your list will be there except for XYZ Company. I understand that their representative, Bob Jones, is on vacation. You might want to get in touch with XYZ and see if they can send a replacement.

Be sure to bring along a box of the brochures we prepared for handouts. I doubt that we have enough in stock here to go around. I've ordered more from the printer, but they won't be ready in time.

Sincerely,

Meeting Recap

Situation   *Taking a few minutes to confirm decisions is a time-saving investment. This memo clarifies responsibilities, prevents misunderstandings, and serves as a reminder to everyone what must be done before the next meeting.*

The Letter   Dear Name:

This will confirm the decisions we made at our task force meeting this morning. You will chase down the user codes and log-ons that we need from Human Resources. I will ask John to get his team organized so that we can begin the data input by the end of the week.

We are ahead of schedule so far but can easily fall behind if the missing information does not get to the programmers right away. Once test data has been input, Sue will be delivering a beta version to XYZ Corporation so they can run bench tests on the system.

Our next meeting is a week from Monday—or sooner if XYZ's testing goes well.

Sincerely,

Negative Report on New Product

Situation   *This letter summarizes reactions on a new product that was recently shown to potential customers. The letter also serves as an outline for a longer, more detailed report.*

The Letter   Dear Name:

We have asked a number of customers and potential clients to take a look at our latest computer system. As part of the demo, participants were given an overview of system capabilities and functions, then encouraged to sit at a terminal and play with the system a little themselves.

So far, twelve people have looked at the system, but only four showed any genuine interest, and these four also expressed concern over the cost. The rest neither returned my questionnaire nor had much to say when I contacted them by phone. I think this negative, or at best neutral, response is a clear signal that we should discontinue development at this time.

I believe our system is as good as any competing product on the market, but if we are to continue development, we should investigate whether we can (a) lower costs without reducing capabilities, or (b) offer enough extra bells and whistles to justify its high price.

Regards,

New Account Application

Situation   *Most businesses include a cover letter such as this one with an application for a new account. This letter summarizes important information asked on the application form. The writer also refers to an earlier conversation with the recipient.*

The Letter   Dear Name:

Thank you for your interest in establishing a new account with XYZ Company. Attached is our application form.

So that we can process your application promptly, please complete all sections on this form. Be sure to include your company's bank account numbers, business contacts, and telephone numbers. We will also need three trade references from companies with whom you presently do business.

You indicated in our conversation that some of your orders may be tax exempt. If so, we must have a signed tax exemption certificate from you on file. If you have any questions or need further assistance, please feel free to contact me at any time.

Sincerely,

New Homeowner Gift

Situation   *This local business makes a point of sending sales letters to new homeowners in town. The letter introduces the services available and offers a free gift.*

The Letter   Dear Name:

Congratulations on the recent purchase of your new home in the Glenview Subdivision. Because this is a new subdivision, once you unpack you will be wanting to landscape your property. We can help.

XYZ Landscaping carries all of the plants, seeds, and tools that you will need to do it yourself. If you would like help, our qualified landscape experts are available to assist you.

One of our most popular services is to have a certified landscape designer draw up a four-year landscaping plan for your property. This plan is free of charge if you agree to purchase all the plantings from us. If you wish, we can also recommend contractors who will do the work for you.

Enclosed is a certificate for a special gift for you, a small potted plant. Please stop by to see us, or return the attached card and we will set up an appointment at your home at your convenience.

Sincerely,

New Member Welcome

Situation   *A professional organization can offer many benefits to those who participate. This letter welcomes a new member.*

The Letter   Dear Business Partner:

It's a pleasure to welcome you as a member of the Local Business Association.

The Local Business Association offers a wide range of programs and services designed to help your business grow. We encourage you to participate in these activities. Those who do discover that the LBA quickly becomes a significant asset to their businesses.

Soon you will receive an invitation to attend a special breakfast for new members. This event is held the first Monday of every month and we urge you to attend. At this time we will introduce you to the many programs and benefits LBA offers its members.

Thank you for your support. We believe the Local Business Association plays an important role in making our community a great place to live and work. We look forward to your participation.

Sincerely,

New Product Announcement

Situation

This announcement introduces a new product line to the sales staff and explains that a previous product has been dropped.

The Letter

Dear Name:

We are pleased to announce that we will be the exclusive distributors for XYZ sound systems. XYZ systems are consistently rated by consumer testing agencies as superior in sound quality, reliability, and design.

A demo system is on its way to you now along with brochures, technical data, and other material for your customers. Many of you have already asked us to start carrying this product, so we're sure that you will share our enthusiasm.

For the last two years we have been marketing QRS sound systems. Unfortunately, sales have been poor due to problems with availability and quality. As a result of these factors and others, we have elected to end our distribution agreement with them.

Sincerely,

New Product Evaluation

Situation   *Clients who examine products in early stages of development are asked for their opinions. The developer is especially interested in hearing from clients who feel the product will have a useful business application. This letter is from a client to the developer.*

The Letter   Dear Name:

Thank you very much for inviting me to see the latest development in telecommunications. Based on what I saw, I think this system may have real potential for my company.

Networking district offices with the main office would have many benefits for us. We would also want to add a camera at each location, specifically for viewing documents.

Thanks again for inviting me to participate. I look forward to receiving more information as the system is readied. If you are looking for a test site, my company would be an excellent candidate.

Sincerely,

New Product Evaluation

Situation   *Developers of new products welcome reactions from potential clients. This client was not impressed with the product.*

The Letter   Dear Name:

Thank you for inviting me to see and try out your new software package.

Although it was most interesting, I am not sure that it would serve our needs. It appears to have many interesting features, although frankly, there are more features than we need now or anticipate using in the foreseeable future.

As you know, we are continuing to evaluate other systems to determine which will be best suited to our particular needs.

Sincerely,

New Product Order

Situation   *This writer is getting organized for a trade show that will be used to launch a new product.*

The Letter   Dear Name:

We are about to introduce our latest product. It's the new model 456, which is manufactured by Smith Company in private label for us. I'd like you to get together with the purchasing department to coordinate our first order of 500 total units.

I will need 50 units for the convention at the end of this month. My intention is to sell as many as I can at the convention. Those that don't sell will be given to the reps to show their customers.

I will need another 150 units on hand when our new ad campaign starts in October. The rest can be ordered as needed to maintain a reasonable inventory.

Thanks for your help.

Sincerely,

New Sales Representative

Situation *This letter is written to introduce a new sales representative. It also affords an opportunity for the salesperson to show some new products in person.*

The Letter Dear Name:

I would like to introduce myself as your new sales rep for XYZ Company.

As you know, XYZ has long been known for excellent service and attention to detail. To make sure that customer needs are being met, representatives like myself are continually updated and trained on new products that can help you. We are committed to giving you the kind of service you need and expect.

XYZ has been listening to what you have to say. We have just added three products that you've been asking for. I will be in your area next week and would like to stop by to say hello and show these new products to you.

Sincerely,

Nondisclosure Agreement

Situation

This memo accompanies a nondisclosure agreement. The writer accepts the need to keep quiet about this business situation, but asks the legal department to approve the agreement first.

The Letter

Dear Name:

Attached is a letter from Bob Smith who represents a small company that might be compatible with our own. That company is for sale.

I'd like to pursue this, but in order to do so, we have to sign the attached nondisclosure confidentiality agreement. It looks okay to me, but I'd like you to look it over before I sign. Note that any disputes regarding this are governed by California laws.

Sincerely,

Notice of Rate Change

Situation   *When rates go up, customers are inclined to ask if the product or service is worth the new cost. This letter justifies the rate change and sells the service again.*

The Letter   Dear Name:

We've had the pleasure of providing services to your firm for the last three years. During that time our prices have remained constant.

Due to increased costs, however, we must increase our rates. In order to continue giving you the best possible service, we must contract with the best employees and use the best materials. For these reasons, we will increase our rates by 7%. Still, we think our price is quite a bargain for the services you receive.

This change will go into effect March 1. If you have any questions, please give us a call. We look forward to continuing to provide the best services available.

Sincerely,

Offer New Service

Situation   *This letter announces a new service for clients. It can be used in several formats, including a press release, a mailing piece, and an offering to current clients.*

The Letter   XYZ Bank is pleased to announce new services for small business owners. We specialize in expert financial planning and asset management. Our goal is to help you find better ways to manage your cash flow. We offer insurance coverage and can guide you in tax and other accounting services. Our on-line services allow customers to check deposit and loan amounts 24 hours a day.

Whether you are starting or expanding your business, XYZ bankers are here to help you. XYZ is committed to providing superior service at affordable rates.

XYZ Bank is open from 8:30 a.m. to 5:30 p.m., Monday through Saturday. On Tuesday and Thursday evenings, we are open until 7 p.m. for the convenience of small business customers. For more information, call 123-456-7890.

Offer Services

Situation   *This letter could be adapted to a wide variety of sales situations. The letter gets right to the point, then offers several reasons why the client should consider the writer's services.*

The Letter   Dear Name:

I would like to help you sell your house!

I understand that you have put your house on the market and are trying to sell it on your own. I respect your decision. As a marketing professional, however, I do want to provide you with some marketing and advertising facts should your initial attempt prove frustrating.

- XYZ Real Estate advertises regularly in all area newspapers and real estate books. This assures our clients that their homes are represented in many advertising sources.

- Increased advertising helps sell your home. The more people who read about it, the more showings you will have, and the better your chances of meeting the right buyer.

- XYZ Real Estate has been the most successful firm in this area for over 30 years. We represent a tradition of sales success.

If you decide to let professionals assist you in selling your home, please permit me the opportunity to speak with you personally. I am enclosing a sample listing agreement for your review.

I look forward to your phone call.

Sincerely,

Opinion Survey

Situation

Surveys offer respondents a chance to give their opinions. The questionnaire and cover letter are sent to several people.

The Letter

Dear Name:

Attached is a survey from XYZ Company, one of our major suppliers.

They are looking for information from us regarding customer satisfaction on their products. This is your opportunity to offer kudos or complaints, so fire away. Your feedback counts.

I'd like these back by next Wednesday. Thanks for your input.

Sincerely,

P.S. If you feel someone else in your department might be better qualified to answer this survey, please pass it on.

Order Delayed Pending Payment

Situation   *If a customer's account has not been paid, you may decide to delay fulfilling an order until the account is paid in full. The letter is short and to the point.*

The Letter   Dear Name:

We have received your order (Purchase Order 1234) for monogrammed glassware.

Because your account is in arrears, we are unable to fulfill this order until past invoices have been paid in full. A statement detailing your outstanding balance is attached.

Your prompt attention to this matter will be appreciated.

Sincerely,

Parking Notice

Situation

When there are more cars than parking places, rules are violated and the employer looks the other way. This notice reminds employees that there are no excuses for breaking the rules any more.

The Letter

Now that the parking lot has been resurfaced and repainted, there is finally enough space for everyone.

Please respect the No Parking signs near fire exits and the loading dock. Spaces near the front entrance are reserved for visitors and handicapped individuals. Employee vehicles parked in these areas will be towed.

Payment Authorized

Situation   *This memo authorizes the recipient to go ahead with a proposed plan. The memo also sets the plan in motion by asking another department to act, too.*

The Letter   Dear Name:

Thank you for your memo of December 3rd. I agree with your proposal that we offer to settle with XYZ 50/50 on the amount in dispute.

By copy of this memo, I am asking the legal department to go ahead and draw up a letter of proposed settlement.

Regards,

cc: Legal Department

Payment Enclosed

Situation   *When sending payment, be sure to say what the check is for. The recipient may be accepting many checks for many different functions. Don't make that person guess which function you had in mind.*

The Letter   Dear Name:

Enclosed is my check for $56.00 for Jane Doe's workshop on October 9th. Thanks for holding my place in the workshop in advance of receiving this check.

I will be attending the October 7th meeting and look forward to seeing you then.

Sincerely,

Payment Enclosed

Situation *This letter accompanies payment. It clearly states what the check is for so that the recipient can process paperwork accordingly.*

The Letter Dear Name:

Enclosed is my SEP contribution for this year (19xx), account #12345. My check for $4,700 is enclosed.

This is a few days late, so I filed a tax extension to make sure everything will be in order. Let me know when the paperwork is completed on your end.

Thanks,

Payment Enclosed

Situation

A transmittal letter doesn't have to be long and wordy. It can be brief and to the point. The idea is to make sure that money is credited accurately. It is possible, after all, that one person will handle your check and another will do the paperwork.

The Letter

Dear Name:

Enclosed is payment in the amount of $1,200. This payment is to cover the following invoices:

- A-312 dated 09/15/xx

- B-645 dated 04/18/xx

- C-978 dated 01/21/xx

Please credit our account, 12345-678, accordingly. Thank you.

Sincerely,

Payment Explanation

Situation   *In this example, a supplier to a retail chain has outstanding invoices and has asked the chain's accounts payable department to look into the matter. The writer has investigated the problem and is telling the customer when to expect payment.*

The Letter   Dear Name:

We have investigated your inquiry of September 18th regarding the following invoices:

No. 1230 dated August 16

No. 4560 dated August 21

No. 8910 dated August 27

We did not receive these invoices in time to make our September 20th check run. Rest assured, however, that the invoices and merchandise have been received and payment will be generated on next week's check run, September 27th.

Sincerely,

Policy Statement

Situation

Businesses have policies on just about everything from credit and collection procedures to who can fly first-class. This policy defines a specific special need and how it will be handled.

The Letter

Standard-sized chairs are provided for all employees. In some cases, however, employees with special needs may request over-sized chairs. Special needs typically include weight over 250 lb. and/or height over 6 feet 4 inches.

Request for an oversized chair should be made to the Assistant Director of Human Resources, John Doe. The requisition can also include a doctor's written request.

If an employee resigns or no longer requires an oversized chair, the chair will be removed and replaced with a standard-sized chair.

Political Support Desired

Situation   *If we expect our legislators to act in our interest, we should make our interests known. In this letter, the writer is asking the legislator to support a certain bill and gives reasons why support is warranted. To find the correct form of address, look it up or call the reference room of your local library.*

The Letter   The Honorable Name
State Legislator

Dear Name:

I am writing to ask you to support Bill 1234. This bill will soon come to a vote in the state senate. For the past five years, it has been working its way through various committees and has been approved by each one.

The purpose of this bill is to help non-dedicated subdivisions in this state. It proposes that one-half of the road and bridge taxes that we now pay be credited to the subdivision in which that taxpayer lives. For example, $250 of my current tax bill is for roads and bridges. Bill 1234 would specify that one-half, or $125, be placed in a special fund to help maintain roads in my non-dedicated subdivision.

I think that this is an important bill. It will benefit the community at large by assisting in maintaining roads that are not normally maintained by a city or county government.

Thank you for your support.

Sincerely,

Poor Performance on Service Contract

Situation

If you have any complaint about service, it is important to document the problem in detail. If there are other significant factors, it may be in your interest to state what they are. In the following case, the work is seasonal and one equipment breakdown can bring an entire job site to a halt.

The Letter

Dear Name:

I am writing to express my continuing dissatisfaction with your company's service on my road grinding equipment. When your mechanic is called, he rarely arrives within the four-hour time period designated by our contract. He also appears to be lacking in knowledge and experience with my equipment.

The short warm-weather season here does not allow for work stoppages and equipment breakdowns. If my contract is to be renewed, we must review the issues of equipment failure, repair personnel, and down time.

Please call at your earliest convenience.

Sincerely,

Poor Quality Product

Situation

Before you make a formal complaint about a product or service, ask yourself if your complaint is reasonable. Was the product faulty, or were you using it in a way that the manufacturer did not intend? Was the service below par, or were your expectations unrealistic? If you feel that your complaint is warranted, try to offer a reasonable solution that might be acceptable to both the business and the customer.

The Letter

Dear Name:

I purchased a Brand X desk from you in August. Since then several problems have come to light. The file drawer on the lower left side sticks. A handle fell off the upper right-hand drawer. The lock on the middle drawer no longer works. Since I have been using this desk only four weeks and it was brand new when I purchased it, I am very disappointed in the overall quality.

Because your job, like mine, requires that you spend a great deal of time at your desk, I am sure you can appreciate the ongoing hassle caused by a desk that continually seems to be falling apart.

As a solution, I am asking that you replace the desk with one of comparable size and features. Two models that seem roughly equal and would be acceptable to me are Model 123 (Brand X) and Model ABC-456 (Brand Y).

Thank you for your help in this matter. I look forward to hearing from you.

Sincerely,

Poor Service Complaint

Situation

Special orders often include extra costs. The additional fee is intended to insure that special attention is given to your order or situation. If you didn't receive the special service for which you paid, you are entitled to complain. Be sure to state the facts, then offer a reasonable settlement. A hostile attitude doesn't solve anything.

The Letter

Dear Name:

This is to confirm our discussion of the problems we encountered with the installation of the custom shelving ordered for our new store. When we placed the order, you assured us that you could do a custom installation for us within the time that we had available. Unfortunately, this did not happen. Instead, these problems occurred:

1. The installation date was supposed to be no later than July 16. The shelving was actually installed on July 19, two days after our store had opened.

2. Our purchase order specifically stated that the shelving was to be installed on the back wall; instead it was installed near the front of the store.

3. Your invoice 1234 includes an extra charge for "rush" installation.

We want to be reasonable and pay for services rendered, but we do feel that you should first move the shelving to its proper place and drop the rush charge from our bill.

Thank you for your cooperation in this matter. We will be expecting your installer here by the end of the week.

Sincerely,

Positive Report on New Product

Situation   *This letter reports that response to a new product has been positive, so development will continue.*

The Letter   Dear Name:

We have been demonstrating our new robotics system to a few of our clients, and the response has been quite enthusiastic, even at this very early stage of development. Of the eleven customers who have seen it so far, nine felt that it had great potential in their industry. They were particularly interested in its applications to shrink-wrap packaging.

I am encouraged by their response and recommend continuing with the next stage of development. I am attaching a budget and a proposed timetable. I have also asked John Doe to research applications in other areas of packaging.

Sincerely,

Potential Sale Follow-Up

Situation   *The salesperson uses this letter to highlight important services that are available. Additional information is enclosed and a visit to the building site is suggested.*

The Letter   Dear Name:

Thank you for taking the time to visit our facility yesterday. I enjoyed talking with you regarding the large atrium that you are considering for the entrance to your office building.

If you decide to proceed with this project, I would like to visit the job site to review critical elements with you. I am enclosing information on the different types of glass that would be most practical for the atrium you have in mind. Our architectural and drafting services will ensure that the design complements the existing architecture of the building.

Thank you for considering us for this project. If you have any questions, please don't hesitate to call. I look forward to hearing from you.

Sincerely,

Preparation for Research

Situation   *Before a research project starts, a preliminary draft of how it will be handled is prepared. This letter asks for any feedback before the actual testing begins.*

The Letter   Dear Name:

Enclosed is our protocol for the comparison study of products that we spoke about yesterday. I am pleased that you will be able to help us with this study and look forward to your comments.

After you have reviewed this protocol, I would like to discuss it with you further. Please feel free to call me with any questions. For the next phase of this study, we will ship the products to you and let you begin your operational tests.

I will call next week to get your feedback about this first stage.

Sincerely,

Product Information Request

Situation   *This letter asks for information that compares one brand with another. Pricing is also a concern.*

The Letter   Dear Name:

Thank you for the information on your products. As we discussed on the phone, I am interested in your floor mats and industrial mops. After looking over your literature, I have several questions about these products:

1. How do your products compare with the floor mats and industrial mops from XYZ? What advantages do your products have?

2. I notice that there are no suggested retail prices in your brochures. Will you send me a price list or do you leave it up to your distributors to set pricing? You mentioned a 10% discount but I must point out that we are currently receiving a better discount from our current supplier. Is 10% the best you can offer?

3. It appears that mops and handles are sold separately. Can they be purchased as a unit?

Thanks in advance for your assistance. Please feel free to call me with this or any additional information.

Sincerely,

Product Out of Stock

Situation   *Thanks to computerized inventory systems, businesses can reduce costs by keeping less inventory on hand than before. As a result, out-of-stock situations are more frequent. Solutions depend on company policy, but here the writer suggests a similar product that can be shipped immediately.*

The Letter   Dear Name:

We regret to inform you that the Model C blood pressure cuff you ordered is temporarily out of stock. We do not anticipate having inventory on this item for another four weeks.

However, we do have two other models that may answer your needs. Model A is the professional model with automatic pressure and digital readout used by many hospitals. Model B is typically sold for home use. I am enclosing brochures on both of these products and hope that one of them will be satisfactory for you.

Unless you notify me otherwise, I will assume that you still want us to ship Model C as soon as it arrives in our warehouse. Thank you for your patience in this matter.

Sincerely,

Progress Report

Situation

This letter reports on the development of a new product. Bullets mark each important point for the reader.

The Letter

Dear Name:

I just wanted to bring you up to date on our progress as we finalize the test prototypes.

- Our engineering department is now preparing final drawings that show how the boxes and transmitters will be fixed to the door frame.

- Programming of the electrical system is proceeding on schedule. We are testing a beta version right now.

- John Doe, Materials Manager, has initiated the necessary paperwork for the product test.

We expect to have twelve prototypes ready for final testing within the month; each of these will be placed in a "live" setting. I will let you know as soon as these are installed.

Sincerely,

Progress Report

Situation   *A work-in-progress report keeps people informed. This report comments on programming issues, the overall schedule, and budgetary concerns.*

The Letter   Dear Name:

Here is where we stand to date on the XYZ project.

1. Dick and Jane have completed the second phase of the program. They are now working with trial data to test the program. There is still some work to do regarding the sales reports that the division managers want. We should be ready to begin inputting XYZ's data in another three weeks.

2. In terms of the overall timetable, we are not doing so well. In fact, we are nearly three months behind the original schedule. There are two reasons for this delay. First, John Doe, who was in charge of this project at XYZ and who was our main contact, resigned just as this project was getting off the ground. At that point XYZ felt that they needed to take another look at this project and evaluate whether they wanted to do it after all. Ultimately they decided to continue, but they made some major revisions to the original specifications. This process was quite lengthy. Second, the original schedule may have been optimistic.

3. The revised specifications do not affect the hardware requirements so, as it now stands, we are well within our budget.

I expect that we will be able to make up about six weeks' time as long as the others involved make their schedules.

Sincerely,

Promotion Announcement

Situation

Promotions are usually the result of hard work, and a company announcement is a nice pat on the back. Announcements clarify new responsibilities and reporting structures.

The Letter

We are pleased to announce the promotion of Jane Doe to the position of Product Manager in the Industrial Equipment Division. Jane joined our company three years ago as a technical representative. She has also held the positions of sales specialist and senior market analyst.

In this new position Jane will be in charge of technical data for laboratory equipment. She will be responsible for researching and developing new market opportunities, including various promotional programs with subcontractors and suppliers.

Please join us in congratulating Jane on her promotion and in wishing her continued success at our company.

Purchase Recommendation

Situation   *This writer requests new software and includes reasons to justify the purchase.*

The Letter   Dear Name:

Per our conversation, this is my official request to upgrade our system software to version 7.0. The cost for this conversion will be $500 per computer, or $35,000. This cost includes software, installation, and licenses.

This upgrade is now essential for the following reasons:

1. We need the supplementary programs that come with version 7. There are several that have been developed to support this version.

2. We need better compatibility with our customers' systems; more and more customers are now using version 7.

3. Our most important customer, XYZ, is making this change. I feel this reason alone justifies our upgrade.

Please order version 7 for my department as soon as possible. Once it is in hand, it will still take several working days to install it on our network and train staff members in its use.

Sincerely,

Quality Control Review

Situation   *This letter announces the schedule for a quality control review.*

The Letter   Dear Name:

Your Beloit operation is scheduled for assessment by the Quality Control Team on August 5, 6, and 7. Our goal is to provide an independent review of your operations in advance of the federal review team, which will be there in November. A detailed agenda for the team's visit is attached. If there are any scheduling conflicts, we can resolve them at our first meeting.

The four team members for this review are listed on the attached schedule. Please provide appropriate escorts for any area where security clearance is required.

Once our review is completed, all findings will be discussed with you at the wrap-up meeting. At that time, we will develop any necessary action plans along with assigning responsibilities and completion dates.

I look forward to seeing you. If you have any questions or concerns, please contact me at the above number.

Sincerely,

Questionnaire Cover Letter

Situation   *Many businesses and professional organizations assess their performance from time to time to identify strengths and weaknesses. This cover letter asks recipients to answer a short questionnaire that will be used for such an evaluation.*

The Letter   Dear Name:

The County Development Committee is attempting to assess its performance over the last five years. We hope to measure our progress, identify areas that need attention, and strengthen the bond between the community and ourselves.

Please complete the enclosed questionnaire. Your candid and thoughtful reply will help our evaluation. Most people are able to complete the questionnaire in less than one hour. Your response and any comments will be treated with utmost confidentiality. After the results are tabulated and compiled, we will issue a report.

Please return the completed questionnaire to us by June 7. A self-addressed, stamped envelope is included for your convenience. Thanks again for your help.

Sincerely,

Rebate Incentive

Situation

This letter puts in writing what the recipient may already know. The letter also affirms that the customer is valued.

The Letter

Dear Name:

We are pleased to offer you the following rebate schedule. It will be in effect for the coming calendar year and will be credited to you at the end of the year. The rebate schedule is as follows:

Sales Growth	Rebate Incentive
1% - 9%	2%
10% - 19%	4%
Over 20%	6%

We value our long business relationship with you and look forward to another successful year.

Warm regards,

Receipt of Unacceptable Substitute

Situation   *If a substitute item was shipped to fulfill your order, it may or may not be acceptable. If not, explain why and how you think the problem might be solved. In any event, you should have been notified before the replacement item was shipped.*

The Letter   Dear Name:

Our recent order for heating equipment has been received. However, a different model was substituted for the industrial heat gun. I am returning it because the substitution is not acceptable.

I ordered model DAC-1 which is your variable temperature heat gun; this gun allows the user to regulate temperatures and hold them constant. The replacement you sent (model DAC-5) is simply a high/low dual temperature heat gun; the user has no control over temperature.

I am disappointed that you made this substitution without consulting us. Please ship as directed on our purchase order. According to Sally Jones, your warehouse manager, model DAC-1 is once again available.

I look forward to receiving the corrected order.

Yours truly,

Recommend Professional Services

Situation *It's good business to develop a network of related services. This letter recommends another professional who can help the customer.*

The Letter Dear Name:

I am enclosing some financing information for you that I received from Mary Smith, loan officer at City National Bank.

There are several ways you can finance the property in which you are interested: 1) take out a second mortgage; 2) get a regular lot loan; or 3) refinance. For more details you'll need to spend an hour or so with Ms. Smith. She is very experienced in real estate financing and can offer sound advice to help you achieve your ownership goals.

After you talk to Ms. Smith, I would be happy to pick you up at the bank to drive you around the area. I'll give you a call in a few days to set up an appointment.

Sincerely,

Recommendation to Discontinue Product

Situation   *Businesses routinely look at their products to decide whether they should be dropped or kept. This letter recommends discontinuing a particular model.*

The Letter   Dear Name:

This will confirm our discussion at this morning's meeting. I think we are in agreement on the two machines that we sell. The larger model is simply not selling and we see no reason for sales to grow meaningfully anytime soon. The smaller units are still a very important component of our overall program.

I think it would be in our best interest to give up the larger units. Even if we do this, we can continue to sell the stock we now have until it runs out. At the current inventory level and if we stop making them today, I think we will be able to offer these to the marketplace for at least another ten months.

Sincerely,

Recommendation for New Procedure

Situation *When making a recommendation, first state the problem, then make a recommendation, and finally, support your point of view.*

The Letter Dear Name:

You recently asked me to look into the matter regarding the fuses that are packaged with the temperature controller.

Model 123, now available, is packaged with a 110V fuse installed. Although the voltage can be changed rather easily, this model does not include a 220V fuse.

With Model 456 now in development, both fuses will be included; 110V fuses will be installed, and we will have a sticker over the voltage switch advising the consumer that when switching voltages, the correct fuse needs to be installed.

It is my recommendation that it will be cheaper to have the manufacturer include the 220V fuse rather than making this an additional step in our final packaging process. Since our ultimate goal is to keep costs down for our customers, we should let the manufacturer supply the fuses.

Sincerely,

Recommendation Letter

A letter recommending a former coworker can be very helpful. Be specific about the person's job duties. If you're not sure or don't remember, ask before you write. Your letter might also be used to verify a portion of the applicant's resume. If you are writing on company letterhead, be sure company policy allows you to recommend a former employee.

The Letter

Dear Name:

I am happy to recommend Mary Smith for employment at your company.

I had the pleasure of working with Mary at XYZ Enterprises in Dallas where she was the Administrative Coordinator of the marketing division. She was organized, efficient, and willing to do whatever was needed to get a particular task finished. Because there were often last-minute deadlines, her cooperative attitude and good cheer were important and appreciated. Although her primary duties were administrative, she assumed some sales duties as well.

Mary deserves serious consideration as a potential employee, and I recommend her highly.

Sincerely,

Recommendation Letter

Situation   *A letter of recommendation from a present employee adds weight to an application. This writer encloses the applicant's resume to make sure there is no confusion.*

The Letter   Dear Name:

Enclosed is the resume for a young man I worked with at XYZ Corp. His name is John Doe, and he is looking for a position here. He recently responded to our ad in the *Daily Gazette* and has been granted an interview with Human Resources on Monday the 14th.

I can personally vouch for his integrity and recommend him highly. If you have any questions, give me a call.

Thanks in advance for your serious consideration.

Sincerely,

Referral Letter

Situation   *This letter is from an employee to the human resources department. The employee is recommending a friend for possible employment.*

The Letter   Dear Name:

A friend of mine, John Doe, will be in contact with you soon regarding a possible job at this company.

I think you will find his credentials impressive and will agree that he has a great deal to offer. If there is a job opening with requirements that match his background and experience, I hope you will consider him seriously.

I would appreciate your letting me know the outcome of your review.

Sincerely,

Reimburse Customer

Situation   *This letter apologizes to a customer and offers to replace the original purchase.*

The Letter   Dear Name:

I want to extend my sincere apologies for the problems you have had with the suit you purchased. The antitheft device should have been removed at the time you purchased the suit. I can well understand your dismay when you tried to remove it but it broke open and stained the suit.

As you pointed out, the device should have set off alarms when you left the store, but it was not working. Because you have the original invoice, we would like to replace the suit. I have set aside an identical suit in your size and will hold it until you can pick it up at your convenience.

Again, I am sorry for the frustration this has caused you and hope that this will set things right. We value your patronage and wish to continue serving you in the best way possible.

Sincerely,

Reimburse Customer

Situation   *Some customer complaints are justified, and so the business tries to regain the customer's goodwill. In this case, the company pays for replacing the damaged item, but also continues its investigation.*

The Letter   Dear Name:

I am as distressed as you are to think that our detergent may have ruined your shirt. In order that we might investigate this problem thoroughly, I am asking that you send the shirt to me so that it can be analyzed in our laboratory. A postage-paid mailing label is enclosed for your convenience.

I apologize for the distress this has caused you. A check for $50 is enclosed to cover the replacement cost of the shirt.

Sincerely,

Reimburse Customer

Situation   *After looking into a complaint, a business may find that the problem was caused by an unusual combination of factors. This letter thanks the customer who first alerted them to the problem.*

The Letter   Dear Name:

At long last we have determined why Part 1234 continued to fail on your car. After much research, we discovered that this particular part has not been insulated for all weather conditions. It does work, but when the wind chill is below -50° F, it will occasionally fail.

We appreciate your bringing this to our attention so that we can fix the problem on other cars. In fact, a recall is now in progress. To show our appreciation, we have made arrangements with your dealer to reimburse you for your last repair.

Thank you again for alerting us so that we can continue to meet our commitment to safety on the highways.

Sincerely,

Reject Applicant

Situation

Applications for employment should always be acknowledged, even if there are no positions available that match the applicant's qualifications.

The Letter

Dear Name:

Thank you for your inquiry regarding employment opportunities at XYZ Corp.

Your qualifications and work experience are impressive, but unfortunately we cannot offer you further encouragement at this time. We will, however, keep your resume on file for six months in case there is an opening that might match your background.

Your interest in XYZ Corp. is greatly appreciated and we wish you every success in achieving your career goals.

Sincerely,

Reject Applicant

Situation   *This is a letter of rejection sent after a personal interview. The recipient is no longer being considered for the job.*

The Letter   Dear Name:

Thank you again for your continued interest in our company.

We have reviewed your resume as well as the additional information that you provided in the interview. Your credentials are excellent, but unfortunately we feel that your qualifications do not match our job requirements. However, we will keep your file active for the next six months in case another opening better suited to your experience develops in the future.

Thank you for your interest in our company. We wish you success in your job search.

Sincerely,

Reject Bid

Situation   *A rejection letter needs only to acknowledge the application and courteously turn it down. This letter also encourages the recipient to try again.*

The Letter   Dear Name:

Thank you for the quotation you submitted to us for our bid for #RJX-604. We regret to inform you that this contract has been offered to another vendor.

We appreciate your interest and would welcome receiving your bid on future jobs.

Sincerely,

Report Follow-Up

Situation   *This letter helps the reader know that the earlier meeting was important, even though brief, and should be continued at a later time.*

The Letter   Dear Name:

I just wanted to follow up on our short meeting this morning. Now that you have the report on last year's product and sales data, I would appreciate it if you would take time to look it over carefully. We need to discuss at length how this information can be used to help improve your marketing efforts.

I will be in town until Monday evening, so I suggest we meet any time Saturday or Sunday. I'm staying at the Holiday Inn on West Main and can meet at a time and place most convenient for you. I'll give you a call tomorrow afternoon to set up a time.

Sincerely,

Report on Lost Business

Situation   *This letter explains why a customer chose a competitor's product. The letter also serves as the outline for a longer report.*

The Letter   Dear Name:

XYZ Company is no longer using our plastic tubing because of incompatibility with one of their processes. They have elected to use a competitor's product because it has an equal life span at a lower cost.

XYZ uses a certain chemical in their inks and glues that evaporates quickly and dissolves just about anything oil-based. Our tubing was adequate but not perfect. After testing our competitor's product, XYZ concluded that it was slightly less expensive and marginally better in performance.

We do have a tubing that is compatible with the chemical XYZ uses, but our tubing is not sturdy enough to stand up to their manufacturing process.

The results of our tests are attached for your information.

Sincerely,

Report Problem

****

Situation   *Reports do not necessarily have to be lengthy. This report gets right to the point and clearly states the problem. Although the report is brief, the programming solution is likely to be complex.*

****

The Letter   Dear Name:

At your request, we have been testing beta version 1.0 and beta version 1.1 of software product X.

We are finding that version 1.0 crashes fairly consistently, particularly if the database is larger than 10,000 entries. Version 1.1 doesn't crash, but the data is often contaminated. It appears to us that the program drops part of the buffer that usually affects the file name.

Obviously, both of these problems need to be solved before we can release the software. Report back to me on what you need to do to fix the problems and how long that will take.

Sincerely,

Request Additional Information

Situation   *Whenever you need additional information, be clear about what you need to know. The writer wants to know what the recipient thinks about a product, and so asks specific questions in order to elicit answers that will be helpful in evaluating the product. If you ask, "What do you think?" and the answer is, "It's okay," you end up with useless data.*

The Letter   Dear Name:

Thanks for sending the information on the Model X machine. I think it might have considerable appeal to some of our customers. However, I do have a few questions.

1. What is the power supply? I am assuming that it requires two 1.5V rechargeable batteries.

2. In your opinion, how does this machine compete with similar units from XYZ Corp. and DEF Inc.? It would appear that your machine is similar to theirs.

3. In your opinion, what are the three most likely applications for this machine?

4. Which markets do you feel are your strongest?

5. If we were to sell your machine through our distributor network, what other outlets would we be competing with?

Thanks in advance for your help.

Sincerely,

Request Additional Information

Situation

Business proposals are sometimes incomplete. This letter asks for additional information and expresses concern about the viability of the overall project.

The Letter

Dear Name:

I received the agency's proposal for revising the auto repair series of books. It appears okay as far as it goes, but there are a number of important questions that need to be addressed.

1. Who is the writer?

2. I think most of the line art is okay as is, particularly the step-by-step diagrams. Who will be providing art for the six new chapters? Will it look the same as the existing art?

3. What about the overall book design?

I think we need to get together with Jane Doe to finalize plans on this. My concern is that much of the information here has already been used in this series.

Call me after you've had a chance to review this proposal.

Sincerely,

Request for Advance Preparation

Situation

This letter to participants sets the stage. The reader is asked to do some advance preparation in order to get the most benefit from the workshops.

The Letter

Dear Name:

Thank you for registering for the training course to be held in Santa Fe on March 17 and 18. This intensive two-day course is designed to help you strengthen your understanding of business strategies. The focus is to develop marketing strategies pertinent to your industry. You will be learning not only from the course itself, but also by associating with managers like yourself from other companies.

The enclosed materials should be read carefully and completed before attending the seminar. The more conscientious you are in preparing for the seminar, the more you will get out of it.

Give me a call if you have any questions. I look forward to getting to know you and sharing marketing strategies.

Sincerely,

Request Appointment

Situation   *If you want to make an appointment with someone you know, it's often easier to call first, set up a time, then dash off a confirmation letter. But if one person lives a long distance away and is only rarely available for a person-to-person meeting, writing ahead is a good idea.*

The Letter   Dear Name:

I understand that you will be in Chicago at the industry convention next month. I would like to get together with you while you're in town so we can discuss the Smith project at some length. I now have some art and samples prepared and would appreciate your input before we go any further.

Let me know what time will be best for you. If you're free Tuesday evening, let's make it a dinner meeting.

Cordially,

Request Appointment

Situation   *If you're asking for an appointment with someone you don't know, then your letter is a way to introduce yourself and explain your visit in advance. You can also use your letter to tell why it would be worthwhile to talk to you.*

The Letter   Dear Name:

I will be in Los Angeles from the 12th through the 16th and would like to meet with you that week.

Enclosed is a brochure explaining the range of services offered by XYZ Corp. As you can see, we specialize in helping manufacturing companies comply with federal environmental laws. To this end, we publish easy-to-understand handbooks that explain in simple terms what is required and provide model policies for you to adapt as you need. Other volumes include the legal cases and court judgments that have interpreted and further defined how these laws are put into practice.

We also offer employee training materials, customized for your particular needs. Our own staff of certified trainers can come on-site to work with your employees, or we can work with your supervisors, showing them how our materials can make their training sessions more effective.

I'll call next week to arrange a convenient time to get together. I look forward to learning more about your business and making a presentation to you about XYZ Corp.

Sincerely,

Request Appointment

Situation   *This customer has a limited amount of time to pursue this opportunity and wants to be sure the salesperson will be available. Customers who express their interest in writing know they will be taken seriously.*

The Letter   Dear Name:

Thank you for sending me the farm listings for my review. I am particularly interested in #3, located in the northwest corner of the county. This parcel is listed at $3,900 an acre; I assume this price is negotiable.

I will be in the area in two weeks and would like to explore this property further. In the meantime, if you have an aerial view available, I would appreciate your forwarding it to me.

My assistant will be calling your office to set up a convenient time for us to meet. Thanks again for your help.

Sincerely,

Request for Business Reference

Situation   *The best recommendation for any business is a satisfied customer. Here, the writer is asking such a customer to put in a good word to a potential client.*

The Letter   Dear Name:

I have had some preliminary discussions with XYZ Company in Nebraska, a printing company you may know. They are building another plant and are considering installing our state-of-the-art heating system. This is the same system that has worked so well for your Syracuse plant.

If you know the CEO or others there, I would appreciate it if you would call and tell them about your experience. John Doe and I are meeting with them on the 15th, so anything you can do on our behalf will be greatly appreciated.

Sincerely,

Request for Changes

Situation

This writer is covering for a coworker who is on a leave of absence. The recipient is asked to forward any ad copy changes.

The Letter

Dear Name:

I am handling the houseware products for Mary Smith while she is on leave. I am unsure whether you responded to her fax regarding the upcoming advertising flyer. Please check to see if there are any changes that need to be made to the current ad.

We are also working on the September inserts for Sunday papers. The listing includes a sampling of the curtains available, and I would like to know if we have omitted any of the more popular styles or sizes.

Please respond by the 25th of this month as deadlines are rapidly approaching. If you have any questions, give me a call at (123) 546-7890. Thanks in advance for your assistance.

Sincerely,

Request for Clarification

Situation   *Many business projects are revised regularly, and each new revision includes areas that need further clarification. This letter requests additional information.*

The Letter   Dear Name:

Thanks for sending the most recent revisions of the electrical schematics and engineering drawings. There are three items that need to be clarified.

1. I am unable to find control valve V-14. Valve V-13 is found on drawings 40D3 and 40D4. Which one is valve V-13? Which one is valve V-14?

2. On page 4 of the schematics, should FCV-21 actually be TCV-21?

3. The oil recirculation pump is controlled by the new computer system now being installed. Per our most recent discussion, you requested that an enable/disable switch be added. However, I do not see this in the wiring diagrams.

I need answers on these matters as quickly as possible in order to keep the installation moving along on schedule. Thanks for your help.

Sincerely,

Request Copy of Report

Situation   *Many organizations will be willing to share information with you as long as you are not competing with them for customers or will not use the data to harm their reputations. Just be clear and, of course, honest about your intentions.*

The Letter   Dear Name:

I understand that your school district conducted a study of attitudes within the community regarding the high school and the various courses it offers. I would like to obtain a copy of this report to use as research for a master's thesis that I am preparing for Western State College.

I would be happy to pay for a copy. If none are available, I would welcome the opportunity to come to your office and study it there.

Thank you for your consideration.

Sincerely,

Request for Different Sales Representative

Situation   *When writing a complaint letter about another person, stick to the business at hand and avoid discussing personality flaws. Criticize the behavior, not the person. Keep in mind that this person is likely to be complaining about you, too. As in any complaint letter, suggest what you think might be an acceptable solution.*

The Letter   Dear Name:

I am writing to express my dissatisfaction with the way our account is being handled.

We have been unhappy with the finished cards because they were not die-cut to our specifications. When we sat down with John Doe, your salesperson, to explain the problem, he seemed unwilling to accept that this was indeed a serious problem. Although Mr. Doe reluctantly agreed to reprint the cards at no charge, his attitude made the situation difficult for everyone involved.

Because of the good service that you have provided to us in the past, we would like to continue having your company do our printing. However, we must insist that a different sales representative be assigned to our account. We feel that most of the current problems could have been avoided if our specifications had been properly documented and conveyed to your printing plant.

Thank you for your attention to this matter.

Yours truly,

Request for Employment Verification

Situation

It is a routine practice to verify information on an application for employment. The potential employee is asked to authorize permission to do this background check. Company policies vary, but many will verify only dates of employment and job titles; they often refuse to reveal salary history or offer information about job performance.

The Letter

Dear Name:

Ms. Jane Doe is being considered for employment at this company.

As part of a routine background check, we would like to verify her employment with your firm. Authorization from her is attached. Please verify her length of employment, job titles, and any recommendation you have regarding her performance.

Thank you for your cooperation.

Sincerely,

Request for Information

Situation   *When requesting information, be specific. Requesting a catalogue may be enough. But if you're searching for a solution to a particular problem, say so. You want facts and advice that will address your dilemma. In this situation, information is needed about carpeting. The writer gives a referral source (an advertisement), asks for information and prices, then very briefly describes the area to be recarpeted.*

The Letter   Dear Name:

I saw your advertisement on commercial carpeting in the April 4th edition of the *Daily Gazette*. Please send a catalog, price list, and information on the different quality grades. This office is looking at several suppliers, as we will be purchasing floor covering for approximately 4,000 square feet in the near future.

In your price list, be sure to include the cost of removing existing carpeting. Are there any other costs (besides the carpet itself and an installation fee) that we are likely to incur?

Sincerely,

Request for Information

Situation   *Requests such as this one are often made by telephone, but it is still advisable to confirm them in writing.*

The Letter   Dear Name:

As discussed today, we are interested in purchasing a large quantity of CD storage racks for resale in our retail outlet. Please send a breakdown of your pricing structure. We are particularly concerned about your ability to meet our shipping dates, as we want to have them in stock in time for the coming holiday season.

I would appreciate hearing from you as quickly as possible.

Sincerely,

Request for Initial Payment

Situation *In some situations, orders can be processed with a verbal go-ahead. In other instances, large orders may require payment in hand before work can begin. The writer is asking for payment and expressing appreciation for the order.*

The Letter Dear Name:

It was a pleasure to receive your signed purchase order today for the installation of XYZ's inventory control system in your warehouse. We at XYZ are convinced this is the right decision and that the estimated capital return on the project will be readily exceeded.

We look forward to working hard on this project to see that it is delivered on time and within budget. Toward that end, we have already contacted our suppliers and subcontractors, asking them to be ready. The installation will start as soon as we receive your initial payment.

John Doe is the supervising engineer on this project and will be handling the day-to-day details. We anticipate no major problems when the system is installed. Please feel free to contact either of us if any questions or concerns arise.

Sincerely,

Request for Interview

Situation   *This writer expresses interest in the company and asks for an interview.*

The Letter   Dear Name:

I have recently relocated to Sacramento and am interested in obtaining employment in public relations. Your company is a dynamic corporation that is known for the challenges and opportunities it offers in this area.

As the attached resume shows, I have extensive experience in arranging conventions and conferences, including expertise in contract negotiations. I am a strong financial manager with well-developed communication skills, both written and verbal. I would welcome the opportunity to meet you and show you some of the brochures, newsletters, and mailings I have prepared in recent years.

Thank you for your consideration.

Sincerely,

Request for Interview

Situation   *A person in this writer's network of business associates has pointed out a possible job opening. The writer asks for an interview.*

The Letter   Dear Name:

Jane Doe told me of your possible interest in hiring experienced executives in portfolio management. I would appreciate a meeting with you to assess how I might contribute to your company.

As shown by my resume, I have an excellent track record in investment and securities management. Most recently I oversaw a portfolio for XYZ Security with a net worth of over $19 million. I am a problem solver who respects the risk tolerance of busy investors.

I will call next week to arrange a mutually convenient date and time for us to meet. During the day I can be reached at 123-456-7890.

Sincerely,

Request from Management

Situation   *This memo makes it clear that advance preparation for the upcoming meeting is required. Since the attendees are all managers, they expect that there will be unspoken competition among themselves.*

The Letter   To: Regional Managers

In order to make next month's sales meeting as meaningful and productive as possible, I would like to address the following issues. Please give the following questions some consideration. The more preparation you do, the more productive our meeting will be.

1. In your opinion, what are our most critical short-term marketing challenges?

2. What are our most critical long-term marketing challenges?

3. In your region, list your most important competitors. In what areas do they compete more successfully than we seem to do?

4. What are the most essential factors for success in your territory: price? distribution? service? quality of product?

5. From your point of view, what are the most pressing needs in terms of contributing to overall profit and growth?

If you are planning to make a presentation, let me know if you'll need special audio-visual equipment.

Request for New Invoice

Situation   *Companies with several outlets often centralize departments such as accounting. This means that suppliers should confirm whether invoices should be sent to the same address as the merchandise.*

The Letter   Dear Name:

Thank you for your inquiry of October 21 regarding payment on invoice 1234.

I have checked into this and we do not have any record of having received this invoice. Since this invoice covers merchandise sent to our Bradford City branch, perhaps the invoice was sent there in error. To insure prompt payment, all invoices should be forwarded to the home office in Atlanta.

Please issue another invoice, addressed to my attention, and I will see that it is processed as quickly as possible.

Sincerely,

Request for Payment

Situation   *This letter accompanies an invoice. It also asks for payment in full right away.*

The Letter   Dear Name:

Enclosed are two invoices. The first is for tuition fees for the twenty participants; the second is for expenses incurred for the training class, including set-up, refreshments, equipment rental, and serving staff.

Thanks for faxing me the list of participants in advance. This allowed me to put together name tags, certificates, binders, and so forth for each individual in advance.

I hope you had a great Thanksgiving, and I wish you a very merry Christmas.

Sincerely,

P.S. Speaking of Christmas, it would be helpful if the checks could be processed quickly to help in taking care of Santa's responsibilities!

Request for Payment Consideration

Situation   *This customer wants to keeps an account in good standing, so suggests a payment plan that will be manageable. The company is likely to accept it, even if reluctantly, because slow payment is better than no payment. Also, the customer is trying to show good intent by not waiting until legal action is threatened.*

The Letter   Dear Name:

As your recent letters have pointed out, I am in arrears to you in the amount of $1,200. Unfortunately, my business has slowed down to such an extent that I am unable to pay in full at this time.

In order to protect my credit rating, I would like to establish a payment schedule. I suggest that I repay you at the rate of $150 per month for the next eight months. Further, I will place no new orders until my account is paid in full. To that end, I have enclosed my check for the first payment of $150.

I hope that this meets with your approval. Thank you for your patience and understanding in this matter.

Sincerely,

Request for Payment Extension

Situation   *Any business can find itself in a cash flow crisis, and small businesses are especially vulnerable. This customer asks for more time to pay, explaining the situation, submitting a small payment, and giving a specific time by which the account will be paid in full.*

The Letter   Dear Name:

I am writing to request additional time to pay the balance owed on my account. Although I normally pay in full each month, my biggest supplier has not yet paid me, so I find myself in a cash flow crisis.

To show my good faith, I am enclosing $300. I expect that I will be able to bring my account current and paid in full within the next 60 days. Thank you for your consideration.

Sincerely,

Request for Product Test

Situation   *This letter asks a coworker to try out the latest attempt to fix a problem. If it still isn't working, it's better to hear about it from a friend than a customer.*

The Letter   Dear Name:

We've gone back and forth with XYZ Corp. about the adapter on their products. We think it is fixed this time around, but we need your help to verify it.

Please install the adapter on the product. I would like to know if it took you several attempts or if you managed to do it on the first try. I would also like your comments on the directions. I know they aren't the best, but are they clear enough? By the way, I am aware of the problem with the drive, but that is a function of the design and it isn't really fixable at this point.

Thanks for your help. Any specific recommendations on improving the installation process and the directions will be greatly appreciated.

Sincerely,

Request to Reprint

Situation   *When asking permission to reprint material, you need to furnish information about where you plan to reprint it and how it will be used. Many authors and publishers will grant permission as long as there is no violation of copyright law. In return, they will likely ask that you include a credit line showing that permission was granted. The standard credit line includes author, title, copyright, publisher, and place and date of publication.*

The Letter   Dear Name:

I am preparing a workshop for city planners, and I would like to hand out reprints of "West Coast Codes Impact East Coast Builders" which appeared in the July 17, 1997 issue of *Industry* magazine. You are widely respected for your knowledge of building and zoning codes around the country, and I think this particular article shows how changes in one metropolitan area often foretell changes elsewhere.

This workshop will be presented around the country, and I expect to reach 700 to 1,000 participants in the next three years. If this is acceptable to you, simply sign the attached permission form and return it to me. If you do not control reprint rights, I would appreciate your letting me know who does.

Sincerely,

Request to Return Borrowed Materials

Situation

Many tasks and situations in business can benefit from a reminder message—to oneself as well as another. In this case, the writer is reminding a coworker that certain materials were borrowed and need to be returned.

The Letter

Dear Name:

In reviewing the list of materials that have been borrowed from my office, your name appears next to the following items:

1. Documentation (1 manual, 1 tutorial guide) for XYZ publishing software. As I recall, you were reviewing them to see if they might be suitable for one of your accounts.

2. Installation disks for QRS clip-art program.

3. A set of small tools in a blue case. You needed these when you installed your new video card and motherboard last month.

Please return these items to my office. If I'm not here, leave them on top of the file cabinet nearest the door. You can also leave them with Mary Smith (her cubicle is next to mine). Call me if you need more time.

Thanks,

Request for Special Billing

Situation   *Most business are willing to accommodate reasonable billing requests as long as you put your request in writing. At the very least, they will give your request serious consideration.*

The Letter   Dear Name:

In an effort to bring our year-end accounts up to date and to a close, I would appreciate it if you could invoice us early, even though the job is not yet completed.

If you're uncomfortable invoicing us for the full amount, perhaps you would consider billing us for the components. Although not all have been installed, I believe everything has been ordered.

Thanks for your help on this.

Sincerely,

Request for Special Consideration

Situation

This customer is asking to have a penalty fee waived, though admits there was justification for the penalty. The business is likely to waive the fee in order to keep this longtime customer.

The Letter

Dear Name:

I have been a VIP customer for three years, and a happy one at that. Two months ago my VIP account was canceled and then reinstated, perhaps because I had made a late payment. At any rate, there is now a $100 penalty on my current bill.

One of your customer service people suggested that because I have been a loyal customer with an account in good standing, you might consider waiving this penalty. As an act of good faith, I have paid the penalty and hope that you will credit my account for that amount.

I plan to continue with you as before as a VIP member. Thank you again for your consideration and service.

Sincerely,

Request for Waiver

Situation

This letter is asking for the recipient to sign a waiver. Because the situation is explained in detail, the reader is likely to cooperate. Letters of this type should be drafted or approved by an attorney.

The Letter

Dear Name:

XYZ Corporation intends to sell its business, including all or substantially all of its assets. Such sale will include the transfer of all intellectual property, including the rights granted to you in 1985. A copy of that license is enclosed.

This letter is to advise you that as stated in Article 12 of the licensing agreement, we are assigning and transferring this license to QRS Corporation, the purchaser. This will be effective on the closing date of this sale to QRS.

QRS has requested confirmation that we have authority to reassign the license to them. Although it is our belief that you are not required to approve this assignment, we would appreciate your signifying acceptance of the assignment by signing the attached document.

Thank you for your cooperation in this matter. If you have any questions, do not hesitate to contact me.

Sincerely,

Reserve Conference Space

Situation *It is good practice to confirm reservations for meeting space in writing so there will be no misunderstandings when the conference draws near. The conference facility itself may issue a confirmation, but if they don't, you should.*

The Letter Dear Name:

Once again XYZ Accounting will be holding monthly training sessions at your facility.

As in previous years, we begin to arrive at 9 a.m. and are generally out of the building by 4 p.m. We will need chairs and long tables (6 ft × 2 ft or larger) for our computers and other materials. There are usually 20 to 25 people plus an instructor in each training session. Allow two people per table; the instructor will need two tables at the front of the room.

The dates are the first Monday and Tuesday of each month, as follows:

October 8-9
November 7-8
December 4-5
January 7-8
February 6-7
March 6-7

A check for $1,200 ($100 per day) is enclosed. We look forward to using your facility once again.

Sincerely,

Resignation Letter

Situation   *When resigning from any position, even a voluntary one, it is good etiquette to send a letter of resignation.*

The Letter   Dear Name:

Please accept my resignation from the board of the Local Business Association, effective today.

Additional business responsibilities are such that I feel I can no longer contribute in an effective manner. I am returning LBA records and files to John Doe. Motions and minutes of the last three meetings have been compiled both in hard copy and on diskette for easy updating.

My experience with LBA has been a most pleasant one, and I have enjoyed working with everyone on the board. As the LBA begins its third year, I wish you and all members very best wishes for continued success.

Sincerely,

Resignation Letter

Situation   *This letter of resignation reveals that the writer is unhappy with recent decisions and no longer wishes to be affiliated with the organization. The writer does not use the letter to preach. The act of resigning is itself a powerful statement. The writer also points out that the differences are philosophical rather than personal.*

The Letter   Dear Name:

Please accept my resignation from the executive board of your organization, effective immediately.

Although I fully understand the reasons behind the new policies adopted by the executive board, I find them unsatisfactory and in good conscience must resign my position. Let me state, however, that I hold no personal animosity toward individual members of the board.

This organization has had a significant and positive impact on the environmental policies of our county. I continue to hold the highest regard for the organization's goals.

Sincerely,

Resignation Letter

Situation   *Sometimes we resign from special-interest organizations because other duties take precedence. This writer has enjoyed participating in the organization's activities and is leaving with some reluctance.*

The Letter   Dear Name:

I am very sorry to tell you that I must resign from the executive board of this organization, effective March 1. I have recently been promoted, and added job responsibilities will take up all my extra time.

My association with this group been long and pleasant, and I wish continued success to everyone associated with it.

Sincerely,

Resignation Letter

Situation   *This writer has enjoyed working for the company; the resignation letter is pleasant. Even if the employee is relieved to be leaving, the resignation letter should not be used to vent frustration and anger.*

The Letter   Dear Name:

Please accept my resignation as Staffing Superintendent, effective Friday, January 18.

I feel very fortunate to have been associated with XYZ Company for the last eight years. My experiences and training have been invaluable, and I leave with many pleasant memories.

Sincerely,

Response to Competition

Situation   *This letter attempts to head off competitors. The recipient is a current customer. The writer wants to caution the customer that it may be too soon for an upgrade because the present system is still adequate and cost-effective.*

The Letter   Dear Name:

With the proliferation of new phone companies, you have probably already been contacted by one of them urging you to replace your existing system. Before you do, however, beware—it may be unnecessary in your case.

Our records show that your present system has been very reliable. You have had only one service call in the last two years and that was due to damage to outside wires after last winter's ice storm. You have also taken advantage of upgrade provisions at bargain introductory costs.

Although it is always worthwhile to review your phone system, we remind you to include reliability records, guarantees, upgrade provisions, and long-term costs in your evaluation.

As part of our ongoing commitment to customers, we are offering free on-site inspections. At that time we would be happy to review your current system and discuss projected needs. Just return the enclosed postcard or call your service representative.

Sincerely,

Response to Complaint

Situation   *After investigating a complaint, this writer tells the customer what the company found out and how they have decided to resolve it.*

The Letter   Dear Name:

As you are aware, we have been investigating your claim with regard to airline tickets purchased last October.

Attached is a copy of the response we received from the airline regarding your problem. We hope this will clarify the situation. There is now a credit on your account in the amount of your last ticket; it will appear on your March statement.

It was a pleasure to be of service. If we can be of any further assistance, please feel free to call me directly.

Sincerely,

Response to Complaint about Customer Service

Situation   *Businesses should always publicly support their employees. Here, the writer acknowledges the customer's complaint and solves the problem, but no blame is assigned.*

The Letter   Dear Name:

Thank you for your letter of November 5 concerning the poor service that you feel you are receiving from John Doe, sales representative.

So that there will be no delay in processing your orders, I have asked Mary Smith from our Customer Service department to contact you. She will expedite your orders and personally see that everything is handled in a timely fashion. Mary is one of our most knowledgeable and experienced sales representatives, and I am sure you will find her expertise to be most helpful.

Thank you again for bringing this matter to our attention. We value your business and look forward to continuing our good partnership.

Sincerely,

Response to Complaint about Quality

Situation   *Quality control is an issue that most businesses take very seriously. Here, the problem was investigated, and the customer service representative explains what happened. A replacement is offered to the customer in order to restore goodwill.*

The Letter   Dear Name:

Thank you for your letter of May 9th regarding the CD player you purchased from us that arrived with a cracked case. We take pride in the way we pack our products for shipping, but in this case it simply wasn't good enough.

You might be interested to know that this is a rare complaint for us, but we received similar ones about the same time. Upon investigation, we discovered that all the damaged CD players were in the same shipment from our manufacturer to our warehouse; they were most likely damaged en route.

We apologize for the inconvenience and are sending you another CD player today. It is the same model that you originally ordered. You may keep the original CD player; the damaged case should not affect its performance. If you decide to throw it away, we urge you to dispose of it in a manner that will protect the environment.

Thank you again for alerting us to this problem. We hope you enjoy your new CD player!

Sincerely,

Response to Customer Complaint

Situation

Sometimes a product fails because the customer is at fault. In the example here, the writer explains what happened, then offers advice to help prevent the problem from recurring.

The Letter

Dear Name:

After you told us that our paint was not adhering properly to the siding on your building, we asked you to send us some paint chips so we could have our experts investigate the problem.

As you can see from the attached lab report, our research department determined that the siding was not prepared properly before the paint was applied. Because the building is very close to a busy interstate highway, there is an excessive amount of road oil and soot on the side of the building. In order for the paint to adhere properly, this oil and grease must be removed first.

Preparation instructions written on the label are quite clear on this point. Directions are highlighted and include a simple drawing to illustrate why careful preparation is so important.

I am sorry that you are disappointed but we do not feel that we are in any way to blame, nor is our product faulty. Therefore, we are denying your claim for reimbursement. We will, however, be glad to send Bill Johnson, our sales representative, to talk to you before you repaint the building. He can recommend specific products which, if used as directed, should solve the problem.

If you have any further questions on this matter, feel free to call.

Best regards,

Response to Customer Complaint

Situation   *Some complaints are easily handled. Here, the writer apologizes to the customer, explains that the service is available after all, and encloses a gift certificate to lure the customer back.*

The Letter   Dear Name:

I am very sorry to learn of your unhappy parking situation at our restaurant last Wednesday. We do indeed have valet parking, but only on Friday and Saturday evenings. However, we are always happy to take care of customers like yourself who desire valet parking at other times.

Enclosed is a gift certificate inviting you to dinner with our compliments. If you will kindly call and let us know you are coming, we will make sure that valet parking is available for you. In fact, any customer who phones ahead can have valet parking any time.

I apologize again for your inconvenience and hope that this will clear up any misunderstanding. We value your patronage and hope that your future meals with us will be fine dining experiences.

Sincerely,

Response to Customer Complaint

Situation   *When a product fails, it is good business to fix or replace it to your customer's satisfaction. In this example, the business admits to the problem and offers to redo the work.*

The Letter   Dear Name:

Our engineers have completed their tests on the concrete breakage on the northwest corner of your parking lot.

They have determined that the concrete batches were mixed incorrectly and, as a result, the corner of the parking lot has not stood up to the weather. Therefore, we are offering to repave that corner at our expense.

Because winter has already set in, we will not be able to make any repairs until next spring. You are at the top of our list, however, and we will repave it as early as possible. I apologize for the inconvenience that this might cause you during the winter, but there really is no option for doing the work earlier.

We appreciate your bringing this to our attention and giving us the opportunity to resolve it to your satisfaction.

Sincerely,

Response to Customer Complaint

Situation   *Customers dislike paying extra money for what appears to be the same product. In this case, the writer explains that the additional fee is due to increased service.*

The Letter   Dear Name:

At your request, I checked on your insurance policy to see why this year's premium had increased. There is indeed a reasonable explanation.

You will be pleased to know that you are paying exactly the same rate for insurance this year as last year. The reason your premium is higher is that you increased your coverage.

When you bought your new truck last year, you increased the liability coverage and added a third driver to your policy. You also added collision coverage that you had not carried on your old truck for the last three years. In short, this year's premium simply reflects the fact that your new truck is worth a lot more than your old truck.

I hope this puts your mind at ease. If you have any other questions, please feel free to stop by my office. It is always a pleasure doing business with you.

Sincerely,

Response to Customer Complaint

Situation

Chances are what the customer says is not the same as what the customer does. In this situation, the manufacturer is unable to explain the problem and takes back the leased equipment.

The Letter

Dear Name:

I am sorry that you continue to be dissatisfied with the machine that you are now leasing from us. As we have discussed, you feel the flow control meter does not give accurate results on this and a previous machine.

We have checked both units very carefully at our facility and they appear to operate as specified. We are unable to explain the discrepancy between your operation and our own.

Please return this unit in its original packing case to our main plant. I am very sorry that we could not help you bring this situation to a more favorable conclusion.

Sincerely,

Response to Customer Query

Situation   *Many older software programs were not programmed to accommodate any calculations beyond the year 1999. This letter assures a customer that the century date change will not cause any problems in this system.*

The Letter   Dear Name:

Thank you for your recent letter regarding potential problems on our computer system when the date changes at the year 2000.

In this instance, there is no problem. The software associated with this product is date-independent.

Please feel free to call if I can be of further assistance.

Sincerely,

Response to Damaged Goods Complaint

Situation   *This letter was written after a customer complained. The supplier looked into the problem and decided to replace the item at no charge to the customer.*

The Letter   Dear Name:

I am sorry to learn that the chair you ordered arrived in pieces. We were able to trace the shipment and even the freight company agrees that the chair had been damaged during shipment.

We are sending another chair to you and it is scheduled to arrive next Tuesday. If you will pack the pieces of the first chair in the original carton and use the enclosed shipping form, you can send it back to us with the driver who delivers the new chair.

We apologize for any inconvenience, but I am sure that you will enjoy the new chair for a long time to come.

Sincerely,

Response to Delivery Complaint

Situation   *As business services become more global and interdependent, a problem in one can affect many. Here, the writer explains what happened. Even when events are beyond our control, we can do our best to make things right.*

The Letter   Dear Name:

Thank you for your letter of July 7th expressing your unhappiness with the late delivery of your recent order—invoice 1234; purchase order R-5678.

We investigated this matter and discovered that your order was briefly delayed at our warehouse and remained on our shipping dock overnight. Unfortunately, this was the night before the XYZ Delivery strike, and all shipments by all carriers were delayed for the next few weeks.

Please accept our sincere apologies for this unfortunate delay. To show our appreciation of your past business, we have credited your account in the amount of the shipping charges on this order. We value our customers and look forward to serving you in the future.

Sincerely,

Response to Employee Complaint

Situation   *This letter is in response to an employee who was unhappy that an available job was given to someone else. After investigating the matter, the writer tells the employee that proper hiring procedures were followed.*

The Letter   Dear Name:

Thank you for your letter of September 5 regarding the position for which you had applied.

We have investigated the matter carefully and we find that the process for filling this position was applied fairly in this case. I appreciate your disappointment and hope you can accept that the final decision was based on very specific staffing requirements.

Sincerely,

Response to Employee Complaint

Situation

Every employee complaint should be investigated very carefully. The complaint may be justified, or a pattern may emerge suggesting that another employee is causing problems. Here, the last paragraph hints that the problem in this case is the employee's own attitude.

The Letter

Dear Name:

After receiving your complaint about unfair treatment, we investigated the situation very carefully. We looked at training and development opportunities in your department and throughout the company. Upon review, we found no evidence of discrimination.

Another training seminar will be offered next month for which you will be eligible. The topic is Improving Customer Relations. I hope that you will take advantage of this opportunity.

Sincerely,

Response to Error Discovered by Customer

Situation   *Errors made in customers' favor are not always mentioned. When errors are reported, be sure to thank your customer and acknowledge his or her integrity.*

The Letter   Dear Name:

We appreciate your letting us know that we included an extra set of kitchen knives, which you had not ordered, in our October 12th shipment (ID-1234).

Please keep these knives with our compliments. An error in our computerized warehousing system caused quite a number of knife sets to be shipped incorrectly, but you were the first to let us know something might be wrong. We are grateful to you for bringing this to our attention.

Sincerely,

Response to Faulty Product Complaint

Situation   *Many businesses set up procedures to investigate complaints from customers. This letter acknowledges the customer's unhappiness and starts the process of trying to discover what went wrong.*

The Letter   Dear Name:

I was sorry to hear that our upholstery fabric is not wearing as it should. We have received only compliments about this line of materials, so I too am puzzled.

Our West Coast sales manager will be contacting you in the next day or two. I would like her to come to your office to inspect the furniture firsthand. At that time, please have ready a copy of your original invoice and the name of your supplier.

We stand behind our fabric and want to resolve this situation quickly. We will keep you posted as our investigation continues.

Sincerely,

Response to Inquiry

Situation   *This letter offers some basic information to the customer, explaining current guidelines for financing. Informed customers are less likely to waste their own or the salesperson's time.*

The Letter   Dear Name:

Thank you for your call yesterday. Your plan for purchasing real estate in this area is thoughtful and realistic, and I will be happy to share information regarding what is on the market. Our office is part of the multiple listing network so we have access to all listed properties.

As a general rule for purchasing vacant land, mortgage lenders require one-third of the total price as down payment. If you plan to build immediately, the loan becomes a construction loan; the requirements are similar to those for a regular mortgage. There are many other factors to consider, of course, and only a lending banker can give you specific advice and information.

I am enclosing several listings along with a map highlighting areas that you might wish to look at more closely. As you know, there are few "bargains" on the market, and reasonably priced homes and lots have been selling quickly.

I will be pleased to line up appointments for you at your convenience. Just give me a call.

Sincerely,

Response to Invoice Error

Situation   *This complaint is easily rectified by sending a revised invoice. However, by apologizing in a brief cover letter, you can restore customer confidence and goodwill.*

The Letter   Dear Name:

Thank you for your letter of June 30th pointing out the error in invoice #1234 dated May 2nd. You are right—we goofed!

We have updated our records to correct the error and a revised invoice is attached to this letter.

Thank you for your understanding, and I hope that you will accept our apologies for any inconvenience this may have caused.

Sincerely,

Response to Job Ad

Situation　　*This cover letter is in response to a classified job ad. The writer attaches a resume, but uses the cover letter to highlight relevant job experience.*

The Letter　　Dear Name:

This letter is in response to the advertisement in today's *Daily Gazette*. I wish to be considered for the secretarial position in the city manager's office.

My employment background and office skills meet the requirements that you are seeking. My experience includes two years working for a state legislator, so I am familiar with the business of government.

I would welcome the opportunity to interview for this position and look forward to hearing from you.

Sincerely,

Response to Job Ad

Situation   *When answering a classified job ad, forwarding a resume isn't enough. You should include a cover letter too. Use it to summarize and draw attention to important information in your resume.*

The Letter   Dear Name:

This letter is in answer to the ad for a paralegal position listed in the job section of the Sunday edition of the *Daily Gazette*. My resume is enclosed.

My legal experience has been varied, involving filings with state and federal courts as well as one brief before the U.S. Supreme Court. I have the ability to work with very little supervision and can effectively establish priorities among competing assignments and tasks.

All aspects of the legal profession are of interest to me, and I would welcome an opportunity to be interviewed for the position you now have open. Your consideration of my application will be greatly appreciated.

Sincerely,

Response to Progress Report

Situation

It is clear that the recipient of this letter will have some explaining to do. Chances are, earlier reports downplayed the issues. It is best to confront difficulties head-on as early as possible. The longer a problem is ignored, the more difficult and more costly the solution.

The Letter

Dear Name:

I read your most recent progress report with great interest. I am alarmed that we are exceeding our budget on this project and there is still quite a bit of work left to do. This should have been brought to my attention sooner.

Please get back to me regarding the reasons why this project is turning out to be so expensive. Before I take definitive action, I would like your input on the best way to reduce costs.

This project will be on the agenda for discussion at our regular weekly Friday morning meeting. Please come prepared with a detailed cost breakdown at that time. Call me if you have any questions or need further clarification.

Regards,

Response to Query

Situation   *The writer followed up on a phone call by writing to the customer. Although the letter summarizes the earlier conversation, the writer also includes another source that might not have been mentioned when they spoke.*

The Letter   Dear Name:

It was nice to talk with you today. I commiserate with your problem of finding current technical data. Many customers find this to be a difficult and ongoing issue.

As we discussed, a good solution would be to check our Web site first. Our on-line information is the most current available. Although we update our printed material regularly, corrections and changes are put on our Web site as soon as we receive them. If we don't have the data, you might also try the manufacturers' Web sites. They sometimes post new data a few days before sending it out.

I think you'll find that files are easy to download from our Web site, but if you have any difficulty, let me know.

Sincerely,

Response to Query

Situation   *This writer is sending information to a customer on disk. The cover letter describes the contents and mentions that the data includes the names of other people who can help.*

The Letter   Dear Name:

The enclosed disk contains the information you requested. Look for filename *partnum.doc*.

This is the interchange list of the manufacturer's part number and the aftermarket equivalent from XYZ Co., QRS Inc., and DEF Corp. You'll notice that the file also includes the names of the people here who handle a particular product line.

I hope this answers your questions. Please feel free to call on us at any time.

Sincerely,

Response to Request for Information

Situation

Replying to an inquiry is a chance for you to make a good impression and open the door to a sale. Take advantage of the fact that a potential customer is interested enough to come to you. Make sure everything you send is up to date and attractively presented. In some instances, you might want to make a phone call first to get more details, so you can fine-tune the information you send back.

The Letter

Dear Name:

Per your request, I am enclosing some carpet samples that should work very well for your company's needs.

The medium gray (XYZ-110) is a good choice for areas where you meet with clients. It is handsome, wears well, and adds a professional look to any conference room. It comes in a full range of colors and designs. Mat 111 (the light pink sample) adds a luxurious, plush feel to this beautiful carpet.

The green and burgundy stripe (DEF-112) is our sturdiest carpet— we think it's practically indestructible! It is an excellent choice for areas that get the most foot traffic, typically hallways and employee entrances. It is easily maintained with industrial soaps and cleaners. You can see from the attached summary report that our lab tests rate it superior to other competing brands. It comes in subtle stripes and multicolor combinations that camouflage all manner of stains and wear. To extend carpet wear, we recommend mat A-02 (the dark pink sample).

Our carpets and mats are priced per square foot, including installation. If your order is over $2,000, we will remove your old floor covering and cart it away for free. Our discount schedule for larger purchases is shown in the enclosed brochure.

Let me know if you have any questions. I would be happy to come to your office to drop off more information or samples.

Sincerely,

Response to Request for Unearned Discount

Situation

When a customer wants a larger discount than usual, you can turn down the request without being negative. Here, the writer simply restates the discount schedule.

The Letter

Dear Name:

Thank you for your inquiry regarding our discount schedule. Our policy is as follows:

Orders under $50—shipping extra

Orders from $51 to $100—free shipping

Orders from $101 to $500—free shipping plus 5% discount

Orders over $501—free shipping plus 10% discount.

Your purchase order D-715 dated June 30 in the amount of $555 entitles you to free shipping and a 10% discount.

Please feel free to give me a call if you need additional information.

Sincerely,

Response to Service Contract Complaint

Situation   *When a customer complains, it is important to address the complaint right away. One unhappy customer can have a negative influence on other potential customers.*

The Letter   Dear Name:

We are very sorry to learn of your dissatisfaction with our service contract.

Sam Jones, supervisor of Customer Service, will be calling to set up an appointment to investigate this problem. He will do his best to resolve this situation as quickly as possible. His phone number is (123) 456-7890.

We value your business and appreciate your willingness to work together with us toward a mutually satisfactory conclusion.

Sincerely,

Response to Ultimatum Letter Sent in Error

Situation   *It is good business practice to acknowledge errors. Customers are more likely to be understanding when you own up to your mistakes.*

The Letter   Dear Name:

You're right—we made a mistake.

Your bill was paid on time, but we had not updated our records properly. As a result, you continued to get letters requesting payment when your payment had been made.

Your records are now in order, and a copy is enclosed for your files. Thank you again for bringing this to our attention.

Sincerely,

Response to Unacceptable Substitute

Situation

Businesses sometimes substitute one product for another when the original product is no longer available. However, most customers want to be asked in advance if this will be acceptable to them.

The Letter

Dear Name:

Thank you for your recent letter expressing your displeasure regarding a substitute item on your purchase order #ABC-1. You ordered desk chair #1234 (a popular basic chair), but instead received chair #5678 (the executive model).

Because the item you ordered was not in stock at the time, we sent a more expensive office chair because we wanted to prevent any inconvenience on your part. This model has several important features that you might enjoy:

- adjustable back
- leather upholstery
- larger wheels and wheel base
- adjustable arm rests

If you continue to be dissatisfied with this chair, please give me a call and I will do my best to help you find another solution to this situation.

Sincerely,

Results of Investigation

Situation

This writer reports on how a problem was solved. The original complaint might have come from a customer or someone within the organization.

The Letter

Dear Name:

In your letter of September 15, you reported that you had found leaks in many of the 2-ounce paint vials that are packaged in kit A-123. The vials in this kit are packaged on a tray.

After investigating this matter, we determined that the problem was due to the wrapping and the placement of the paint vials on the tray. We have redesigned the packaging so the paint vials are better protected. We are confident that this will solve the problem.

We appreciate your taking the time to make us aware of this situation. Your concerns and opinions are essential to our goal of producing the highest quality paint products.

Sincerely,

Resume Cover Letter

Situation *This applicant uses the cover letter to highlight relevant experience and ask for a personal interview.*

The Letter Dear Human Resources Director:

I am pleased to respond to your advertisement in the *Daily Gazette*. I am seeking a long-term position in an educational environment.

As the enclosed resume shows, my experience includes recruitment scheduling, travel arrangements, articulate correspondence, budgetary and financial management, plus excellent organizational skills. I am familiar with and currently use the popular word processing, spreadsheet, and database programs; my computer abilities are exceptional.

I would welcome the opportunity of a personal interview because I feel I have the depth of experience you are seeking. I look forward to hearing from you.

Sincerely,

Resume Cover Letter

Situation

When answering an ad, make sure you send a cover letter with your resume. Use the letter to show that you are uniquely qualified for the position.

The Letter

To Whom It May Concern:

I am writing to apply for the position of convention manager described in your ad in the Sunday *Daily Gazette*. As the attached resume shows, my strengths are organization and communication. My responsibilities have included the complete execution of large exhibits and trade shows, meetings, conventions, and seminars in numerous locations throughout the U.S.

My communication experience includes writing brochures, newsletters, press releases, and meeting minutes. I am also an accomplished public speaker and trainer. Most recently, I was in charge of the national conference for an international public speakers' association. Currently I serve as regional president of this group.

I also have extensive supervisory, financial, and accounting experience. I am a strategic thinker who plans details and contingencies in advance. As a team player, I enjoy working with both paid and volunteer staff to accomplish mutual goals.

I believe I have the skills and experience you seek and would welcome the opportunity to discuss your requirements and my qualifications.

Sincerely,

Retirement Congratulations

Situation   *Most people see retirement as a reward for having worked long
and hard at a job. For some it signifies the end of one career and
the beginning of another. For others, retirement is the beginning of
a more relaxed lifestyle and the opportunity to pursue personal
hobbies and dreams. At the very least, retirement is a milestone in
one's life and deserves recognition.*

The Letter   Dear Name:

Congratulations on your retirement from XYZ Corporation. Their
expertise in database programming is a testament to your abilities
and knowledge of management information systems.

I understand you and [spouse] will be moving back to California
this fall. I'm sure you'll enjoy being able to devote more time to
restoring antique automobiles once you've resettled near your old
hometown again.

You'll be missed at XYZ, but everyone wishes you happiness and
joy in your retirement.

Sincerely,

Sales Call Follow-Up

Situation *When calling on one customer, you might very well meet other people involved in the project. It is good practice to write a brief letter to those people too, particularly if you think they might be playing a larger role in the future.*

The Letter Dear Name:

It was very nice to meet you last week while I was showing our new floor coverings to Mary Smith. XYZ Kitchen Designs has always had a good reputation and clearly it is only going to get better. Our company is quite pleased to be one of the vendors whose products are used in your new showrooms.

The new designs Mary showed me are excellent and beautifully done. It is interesting to see what you and she are doing. Keep up the good work!

Sincerely,

Sales Call Follow-Up

Situation

Writing a letter after you've made a sales visit is a must. First, your letter will extend an important courtesy, one that is too often overlooked today. You can say thank you "for taking the time to meet with me," "for listening to my presentation," "for telling me about your business." Second, your letter is a chance to review what was discussed, recap what you learned, and restate your sales pitch. Finally, your letter can keep things moving—you can initiate an action, invite a response, ask for the order.

The Letter

Dear Name:

Thanks for taking the time to listen to what XYZ Printing has to offer. I realize that you are under contract with another vendor at this time, but I hope you will consider Acme in the future. As you know, our pricing structure is competitive and we take pride in our ability to handle rush jobs.

XYZ, of course, is interested in printing your next catalog. Once your decisions on the new design and page specifications have been finalized, we will send our quote to you. XYZ has long been known for our service to customers, and our account supervisors are always willing to share their knowledge and experience in order to make your job proceed easily and smoothly.

I'll give you a call around the 25th of the month to see if the specs are ready. I look forward to further discussions with you.

Cordially,

Sales Call Follow-Up

Situation

If you didn't make a sale this time, you want to be on good terms with this potential customer so that you'll be in the running for future business. If this person isn't in the market for your product or service, he or she might recommend you to someone who is. Also, this person might eventually take a job somewhere else where your services are needed.

The Letter

Dear Name:

Thanks for taking the time to see me today and to take a look at the engineering consulting services we now offer with our exclusive metalizing process.

I understand that you are satisfied with the suppliers you work with now, but if a special need arises in the future, I hope you will consider XYZ Metals as a source.

Thanks again.

Cordially,

Sales Call Report

Situation

Salespeople document their sales visits using call reports. These reports are important as reminders of what took place and what should be done. In this instance, the salesperson learned that a potential market was opening up and who would be in charge of it.

The Letter

I called on John Doe today at XYZ Corp. and met with him for about half an hour. He told me that they have been thinking about advertising in several small specialty catalogs rather than one large annual one. They will probably break up their lab equipment into smaller catalogs—one for slow meters, one for heating equipment, another for material handling, and so on. He did not expect to have much direct involvement and thought Mary Smith would most likely be appointed to head up this change. I have made an appointment to see her in two weeks.

Sales Follow-Up

Situation   *It is good practice to write a letter after meeting a potential client. You can use your letter to sell yourself and your business one more time.*

The Letter   Dear Name:

It was very nice meeting you when I was in Atlanta last week. I am enclosing some material on several of the projects that we discussed, including two articles that I wrote for our corporate newsletter on the stock market and a proposal for a series of articles on retirement planning.

I think you will agree that my qualifications are well suited to your needs. I would like to meet with you to discuss financial investment seminars for your corporate executives.

Thanks again for your courtesy. I'll call you next week to set up a convenient time for our next meeting.

Cordially,

Sales Follow-Up

Situation

Every order is an opportunity to make your customer pleased or annoyed. If the order is handled with care and attention, the customer will come back again, perhaps placing a larger order next time. If the order is from a customer who uses your products or services regularly, it's easy to take that business for granted. Make sure steady customers receive the same care and attention as new customers.

The Letter

Dear Name:

I'd like to take the occasion of your recent order to thank you again for your continuing business. It has been most gratifying to watch each of our businesses grow, along with the spirit of cooperation and partnership between us.

XYZ is proud to be your auto parts supplier. We value our relationship with you and look forward to many more years of serving your needs.

Sincerely,

Sales Follow-Up

Situation

This letter is a follow-up to a previous sale. The recipient has already purchased the core product, and the writer now wants to interest the buyer in supplementary materials.

The Letter

Dear Name:

You have been using our social studies books and workbooks in your classrooms for the last semester. Like other educators, you have found these very useful in your social studies programs. Teachers and students alike are pleased with the new layout and the clear way in which information is presented.

Now is the time to think about ordering the corollary materials—overhead transparencies, slide sets, and videos—that go along with the text. These materials are designed to enrich the original textbook series, but they also work very well as stand-alone teaching aids. Many schools buy one set of slides, then share them among all teachers in the department.

I am enclosing our catalog and price list. When ordering workbooks for next year, consider adding one or more of these useful supplementary materials to your order. I'll be calling you in a few days to answer any questions you have.

Sincerely,

Sales Lead Follow-Up

Situation   *A smart salesperson pursues every lead, knowing that some of them turn into sales. This letter is a follow-up to a phone inquiry; the writer offers to deliver additional information in person.*

The Letter   Dear Name:

I enjoyed talking with you this morning and sharing some of the exciting things that are happening in this area.

As you know, Route 10 is a prime artery into this county and a major interchange off the interstate. Commercial investment parcels are still quite reasonable in this area, and I think your goal of moving your company here is a sound decision.

Because your schedule is quite busy, I suggest that I visit you at your office and bring along maps and collateral materials regarding acreage for sale in this area. When we get together, I can also share the latest information from the planning and zoning office.

Give me a call and we'll set up a schedule at your convenience, hopefully as soon as possible. I look forward to hearing from you.

Sincerely,

Sales Letter

Situation *This letter does a good job of selling training seminars and summarizes important information that is enclosed.*

The Letter Dear Name:

Thanks for your interest in our product manager's seminars. Attached is a list of clients for whom we have done seminars in the past. You will note that seven companies have been so pleased with the results that we have returned to do additional seminars.

Course 101 is designed primarily for new product managers—those with less than 18 months on the job. The focus is on principles of marketing.

Courses 201 and 301 are designed for a cross section of managers, including those from marketing, sales, research and development, manufacturing, and so forth. In fact, we have found that these courses are most effective when key departments participate with each other.

Course 401 is on leadership training. It is a new course and the word is just getting out, but the feedback on the seminars we've presented so far has been excellent.

I am looking forward to discussing these programs in greater depth with you when we meet next week. I think you'll find they can be very helpful in meeting your career development objectives.

Sincerely,

Sales Report

Situation   *This sales report is concise and well organized. The headings make it easy to read and follow.*

The Letter   SUBJECT: XYZ Distributors

Sales Analysis

XYZ Distributors is located in the southern part of the state. They service 19 counties; most of their business is agriculturally related. Due to the unusually severe weather, earthquakes, and fires, these agriculture industries were severely affected. In fact, much of the area that XYZ services was closed down due to mud slides and flooding.

In addition, XYZ's most experienced salesperson resigned.

Current Programs

A new salesperson has now been hired and is being trained. XYZ is also talking to mailing list companies to find a more productive list, as their most recent effort was a complete flop.

New Programs

A sales contest—brand new to XYZ—will start May 1 and will continue through the end of August. I am also setting aside one day each week to train new people and accompany them on field calls. We are working hard to generate new business that is not agricultural. A new mailing should be released within six weeks.

Projected Sales Estimate

In spite of the weather problems, XYZ Distributors should remain at or slightly above last year's sales.

Scholarship

Situation   *Companies that support education are making an investment in the community as well. This business is announcing a scholarship to be used toward college tuition.*

The Letter   We are pleased to announce that we are sponsoring a $1,000 scholarship to be used toward college tuition.

One scholarship a year will be awarded to a graduating high school senior. Any student whose parent or legal guardian is currently employed here is eligible. Other requirements include academic scholarship, good citizenship, and a written essay.

For more information contact the high school guidance department at 123-4567.

Seminar Announcement

Situation

Many organizations and companies offer training sessions and seminars. These continuing education programs offer new ideas and inspiration to businesspeople and other professionals.

The Letter

Dear Name:

The Local Business Association is proud to announce that they are sponsoring a series of seminars for local business leaders. These seminars are designed for business owners and their associates who wish to advance in their professional field. Representatives from government and civic organizations will be in attendance as well.

The enclosed brochure gives a detailed description. A single fee entitles you to attend all five programs this year.

To make reservations please call the Business Association office. I urge you to act quickly as there are only a few openings left for this year's series of seminars.

Best regards,

Service Provider Request

Situation   *This business is notifying the customer that payment is expected for service. The letter is pleasant and avoids a "gotcha" tone.*

The Letter   Dear Name:

Our records show that cable TV is being used at this address. Apparently there has been an oversight or misunderstanding because this account has not been put in your name. We would appreciate the opportunity to provide the service and welcome you as a new customer.

If you wish to establish cable TV service in your name, please call this number or visit one of our offices. If we do not hear from you by next Friday, we will assume the cable TV is no longer needed and we will discontinue this service.

Thank you for your cooperation.

Sincerely,

Shipment Sent Separately

Situation   *If a package of material is being sent, a packing list should be included in the box to verify the contents and recipient. However, if the package is going to a large company, you also might want to notify the recipient with a separate letter. Packages have been known to spend extra hours or days in company shipping departments.*

The Letter   Dear Name:

This is to let you know that two cartons of radio components were shipped to you this morning via Appalachian Express, tracking nos. A-1234 and A-1235. They should arrive before noon on Thursday.

The contents are packaged as follows:

    A-1234: outer cases, knobs, and panels

    A-1235: antenna wire, crystals, and receiving chips

I'd appreciate it if you would give me a call when you have them in hand.

Sincerely,

Smoking Cessation Classes

Situation

In order to promote employee wellness, this business is sponsoring a smoking cessation clinic for employees who use tobacco products.

The Letter

As many of you know, the city has announced that in two years all public buildings will be smoke-free. We have agreed to adopt this policy too.

The dangers of smoking to both smokers and their families are well documented. We have invited the American Lung Association to run a series of smoking cessation seminars for all interested employees. This four-week course is designed to help you stop smoking for good.

The cost of the course is $50, but if you stop smoking, it's free. We will reimburse you for the cost of this course on your one-year nonsmoking anniversary.

You know you've been wanting to stop smoking for a long time now. This is your chance. Classes start next Monday in Conference Room A at 12 noon. A box lunch will be served to all those attending.

Special Offer to Current Customer

Situation   *Many businesses encourage upgrades of services to existing customers. In this instance, a renewal membership entitles the customer to a special add-on offer.*

The Letter   Dear Name:

Thank you for renewing your single membership in the XYZ Health Club. In order to show our appreciation, we have some great news for you.

You now qualify for a special discount on a family membership. Sign up the rest of your family for one year and the first two months are free for them. The details of this special offer are explained in the enclosed brochure.

If you have any questions, give me a call.

Sincerely,

Specifications List

Situation   *When discussing specifications on any project, it is important to be clear and concise. Numbering each point creates a handy checklist.*

The Letter   Dear Name:

I am enclosing the materials that we're using now. The brochure we discussed definitely needs to be redesigned. Here are some of the points we discussed:

1. The return address on the 9 × 12 envelopes is too small.

2. The #10 envelopes look dated. (Frankly, I never did like this stock.)

3. Beckman Old Style font, which I do like, is used on some pieces.

4. Critique sheets from the last conference are attached. You should be able to pick up some good quotes from these.

5. I am open to suggestions on color and style as long as it is attractive and professional in appearance.

I'm looking forward to seeing your sample mock-ups on this material.

Sincerely,

Status Report

Situation   *This memo is a status report on fences. It also includes relevant data needed for the purchase order.*

The Letter   Dear Name:

Attached is a table outlining the kinds of fencing we will be using for the new construction at Plants #3, #4, and #7.

- Fencing for Plant #4 is the standard construction fencing; it will be purchased first and by the end of this week.

- Fencing for Plant #7 is a more elaborate railing system; it will be ordered by the end of the month.

- Restraint systems for the other plants are minimal and will be included in the Plant #7 order.

For your convenience I have included part numbers and prices on the enclosed chart. You'll need this information for the final purchase order. Let me know if you have any questions.

Sincerely,

Strong Request

Situation   *Avoiding contact usually makes resolving a problem even more difficult. Here, the writer is annoyed and is unlikely to be in a compromising mood.*

The Letter   Dear Name:

If we are to make any headway in resolving the manufacturing issues, we need to discuss the matter at length and in detail.

However, I am having a great deal of difficulty reaching you. I have left three voice mails per day for the last week. I have also asked your assistant to tell you that I consider your return phone call a requirement if we are to work together.

Call the office any time. If I'm not at my desk, ask the operator to page me. Contact is essential if this professional relationship is to continue.

Sincerely,

Summary of Findings

Situation

This letter is the summary of an investigation. If expanded into a lengthy report, the writer should change the numbered items to headings for easier perusal by readers.

The Letter

Dear Name:

At your request, I've been looking into the problem of finding extra space for this company. I feel there are three possibilities, though none is perfect. In my order of preference, these are:

1. Add on to the existing building. The logical place to do this is on the north end of the building. The problem is that we will lose one-half of the parking lot and will need to lease parking space nearby.

2. The XYZ building on East River Street is for sale, and we could move our warehouse into that facility. However, the price is high. Also, there will be some resistance to this idea because many departments now benefit by having the warehouse connected to the plant.

3. QRS Industries have announced they are moving to Arkansas. Their local facility is now available at a bargain price. The difficulty here is that we cannot assume occupancy for another twelve months, and the space is more than we need at the present time.

I'm doing a presentation on this at the management meeting next Monday, but would like to discuss this with you ahead of time. Please give me a call at your earliest convenience.

Regards,

Summer Hours

Situation   *Certain industries have special hours during the summer. This notice explains the new hours and reminds employees to respect the privilege.*

The Letter   To All Employees:

New summer office hours will be in effect starting Memorial Day and ending Labor Day. We will open one hour earlier (8 a.m.) Monday through Friday. We will close at 12 noon on Friday. These hours are in keeping with other companies in our industry.

Please bear in mind that we consider this summer to be a trial period. If this privilege is abused, then regular hours (9 a.m.-5 p.m.) will be in effect year round.

Summer Intern Position

Situation   *This job offer is for a summer position. The letter includes both the starting and ending dates. It also states that the recipient will have to sign a confidentiality statement. Many businesses guard proprietary information very carefully.*

The Letter   Dear Name:

We are pleased to offer you a position as a summer intern in the Photography Department. This program starts on June 15 and ends on August 15.

On June 15, please report to the Human Resources Department to process the necessary paperwork. Because you are likely to have access to proprietary information, you will be asked to sign a contract stating that you will not disclose this information nor use it to benefit another company. Signing this confidentiality statement is a condition of your employment.

We are pleased that you have decided to participate in our intern program and look forward to seeing you this summer.

Sincerely,

Supplier Problems

Situation   *Business is conducted internationally today, and import/export regulations can complicate a situation.*

The Letter   Dear Name:

We have been having problems importing a special optics grinder. The reason is that it is classified "dual use" by the European trade authorities. That classification reflects the concern that this product could be used in making weapons of mass destruction.

Today I learned that our supplier has decided to stop importing it. Their problem is that they now have to vouch for every customer to whom they sell this equipment. We're just trying to make eyeglasses, but who knows what the next customer has in mind.

We're now searching for another supplier. However, because this equipment is so highly specialized, we're having a hard time finding a suitable alternate.

Regards,

Survey Cover Letter

Situation   *This survey is designed to make it easy for the reader to reply. A crisp dollar bill gets the reader's attention.*

The Letter   Dear Customer:

Your input is needed on a new product now being developed. Because you are a purchasing agent or buyer, your opinions are important.

This new product is pictured on the reverse along with a description and list of questions. After answering the questions, simply return this survey using the pre-addressed stamped envelope. Feel free to add your personal comments. Your answers will be kept confidential and will be used only in combination with other replies.

Thanks very much for your help. The attached brand new dollar bill is to brighten the day for a special youngster in your life.

Sincerely,

Technical Modification

Situation

This technical modification is easy to follow. Steps are numbered, and the work is explained in straightforward language.

The Letter

Technical Modification

The following modification is recommended for receiver model 123. This modification will allow for radio reception above 88 MHz.

1. Remove cover.

2. Locate diode X-456. It is just to the left of the filter. You may need a magnifier and tweezers.

3. Using a soldering iron, heat each diode very carefully.

4. Using tweezers, lift and remove the diode.

5. Replace cover.

6. Turn on receiver and reset microprocessor.

Termination Agreement

Situation   *This letter confirms an agreement with the employee regarding repayment of a hiring bonus.*

The Letter   Dear Name:

When you were hired last July, you were awarded a sign-on bonus. As part of your contract, you agreed to repay this bonus if you left the company on or before 18 months from your date of hire.

Per our discussion yesterday, we agreed to prorate your bonus over 18 months so that you could repay the bonus only for those months that you had not worked. We also agreed to deduct this amount from your accrued vacation pay. A detailed calculation is attached.

If this option is acceptable to you, please sign the attached agreement and return it to me. Upon receipt we will process your check.

Sincerely,

Thank You with Apology

Situation   *Unfortunately, some people behave inappropriately. In this case, the writer apologizes for another's rude behavior.*

The Letter   Dear Name:

I just want to thank you again for coming to speak to our organization. Your lecture and slides were interesting and informative, and the workshop was excellent. Your lecture was a grand way to start our organization's year.

It was brought to my attention that one of our members was out of line the second day of the workshop, and those present were quite embarrassed by his behavior. I want to apologize personally and on behalf of our president as well as the rest of our organization. Please accept our sincere regrets, and I hope that you will remember our group by the attention and enjoyment that everyone else displayed.

You are a generous and inspiring lecturer. Thanks again for sharing your talents and knowledge with us.

Very best wishes,

Thank You for Business Referral

Situation *When a business associate from another company recommends your services to a customer, be sure to say thank you.*

The Letter Dear Name:

Thanks for suggesting XYZ Metal Company to John Doe. As you suspected, his project will require customized slotted tubing, one of our specialties.

Thanks again for recommending XYZ Metal to your customers who need metal roll forming and stamping. We value your endorsement, and we shall continue to do our best to satisfy their needs.

Sincerely,

Thank You for Donation

Situation   *Donations should always be acknowledged. This donation was a needed item rather than money.*

The Letter   Dear Name:

Thank you very much for donating the two covered sand tables to the nursery school.

The children are already hard at work—sifting, pouring, digging, and playing. Because of your generosity, the children are able to play with sand indoors where we can keep the tables clean and covered when not in use.

Enclosed are some photos of the children playing at the sand tables. As you can see, they are having a wonderful time. Again, we appreciate your thoughtfulness.

Sincerely,

Thank You for Favor

Situation   *Much of our education comes from other people. Here, the writer thanks a business associate for sharing expertise and offering worthwhile suggestions.*

The Letter   Dear Name:

Thank you for taking the time last Thursday to share your technical knowledge and experience with color printers. After talking to you, I had a better idea of where this technology is headed.

I took your advice on the kinds of questions I should be asking different manufacturers and how to go about evaluating our in-house needs. It became obvious that in some departments, a color printer is a requirement; for others, it represents unnecessary bells and whistles.

Thanks again for your expertise and help. Whenever I can return the favor, please let me know.

Best regards,

Thank You for Hospitality

Situation   *Thank-you letters are essential, and sadly, too often neglected. An expression of gratitude in writing reinforces what you might already have said in person. A thank-you letter is a quiet, thoughtful message that will make your reader feel appreciated.*

The Letter   Dear Name:

I just want to thank you again for your hospitality while I was in Chicago last week. You were very nice to show me around the city. The trolley-car ride was a great way to see the highlights, and I only wish there had been time to get off at each stop. Dinner at the top of the Hancock Building was a special treat. It was a beautiful clear night, and the view was spectacular.

Thanks again for a wonderful afternoon and evening. Now I understand why you say you'll never live anywhere else.

Sincerely,

Thank You for Hospitality

Situation   *Many people use social occasions to promote business interests. Here, the writer expresses appreciation for a relaxing evening where business was discussed.*

The Letter   Dear Name:

Thank you so much for your generous hospitality when I was visiting last week. The dinner party at your home was relaxing and enjoyable. It gave me a unique opportunity to get to know Mary and Bill better. We even discussed a preliminary schedule for the forthcoming XYZ project.

I assume that you will be coming this way for the QRS convention next fall. I hope I can return the favor and show you around our fair city.

Best regards,

Thank You for Interview

Situation   *Show professional courtesy by writing a thank-you letter to your interviewer. Use the letter to indicate your continued interest in the job.*

The Letter   Dear Name:

It was a pleasure speaking with you today and discussing the job opening now available in your customer service department.

The parameters of the job as you described them were most interesting, and I feel that I am uniquely qualified to fill this position. I certainly remain very interested and look forward to hearing from you at your earliest convenience.

Thank you again for your time and courtesy.

Sincerely,

Thank You for Professional Assistance

Situation When you benefit from another's hard work and professional expertise, be sure to thank that person.

The Letter Dear Name:

I want to take this opportunity to thank you for the time and interest you have taken in our case. As you know, for the past two years we have been writing letters and filling out forms with Social Security regarding the omission of our payments while we were living abroad. But until you accepted us as clients, we had had no success in getting the problem resolved.

Thanks to your expertise and assistance, the matter has finally been resolved.

Sincerely,

Thank You for Reference

Situation

It is important to thank references. If the person has been contacted numerous times, he or she has gone to some trouble on your behalf.

The Letter

Dear Name:

I thought you would like to know that I have been hired as training director for XYZ Corporation. The job is going to be quite challenging, but I'm looking forward to starting next week.

I want to thank you again for your recommendation. Your kind words were important in helping me land this job.

Best wishes,

Thank You for Referral

Situation   *Personal referrals often open doors to new business. Be sure to express your thanks to someone who recommended you.*

The Letter   Dear Name:

Thank you for giving my name to Bob Jones as someone who might be interested in developing material for his financial newsletter. Bob and I have already scheduled a second meeting and at least one project looks quite promising.

I appreciate your recommendation and will work hard to make sure that your kind words about me are indeed true.

Best personal regards,

Thank You for Service

Situation   *A letter praising an employee may do more good than you know. The employer will at least be aware of a good employee, and your letter may even tip the scales in favor of a better raise.*

The Letter   Dear Name:

I want to thank you for the efficient and expeditious manner in which my recent application was handled. In particular, I would like to commend Ms. R. Smith.

Ms. Smith was very thorough in our initial conference, saving us unnecessary meetings and repetitious steps. She is a good spokesperson for your department.

Sincerely,

Thank You to Speaker

Situation   *Writing to a speaker is a nice gesture. Your speaker worked hard to present information in an interesting way and will appreciate your kind words.*

The Letter   Dear Name:

The presentation you gave yesterday on Understanding Medicare was very helpful. I learned a great deal and plan to follow your suggestions. The material you distributed will be most helpful, and I look forward to sharing it with several friends who were unable to attend.

There is a definite need among senior citizens to become better informed on this topic. Your seminar provided an excellent forum for us to ask questions and voice opinions.

Thank you again for such an informative and pleasant afternoon.

Sincerely,

Thank You for Suggestion

Situation

Thoughtful suggestions should be acknowledged. This letter recognizes that the suggestion is valid and may be implemented at a future time.

The Letter

Dear Name:

Thank you for your recent letter suggesting that we keep our store open twenty-four hours.

This idea has come up from time to time and in fact has been implemented successfully in some areas. For this store, however, we feel that we do not have enough overnight customers to offset the additional operational costs.

Thank you again for your thoughtful comments. We appreciate your interest in letting us know how we might better serve our customers.

Sincerely,

Thank You to Subcontractor

Situation   *When work is subcontracted to another, you are pleased when their work is as good as your own. Express your appreciation in writing because you may want to hire them again.*

The Letter   Dear Name:

This is to tell you how much we appreciate your help last month. We were able to fulfill every paving contract before the cold weather set in, so we didn't have to turn anyone down. This was possible only because we could subcontract some of the work to you, knowing that your standards were equal to our own.

Thank you very much for your professional services. Your reputation for quality is well deserved.

Sincerely,

Thank You to Team

Situation   *This writer is letting a team know that their work is recognized and appreciated by many others.*

The Letter   Dear Name:

I just wanted to thank everyone who is involved in the Santa Fe project. A total of 730,932 units were repackaged and relabeled on time—and the final cost was 24% below the original estimate. Your group did an absolutely phenomenal job!

Thanks from all of us in the home office.

Best personal regards,

Third-Party Complaint

Situation   *Not all complaint letters come from customers. In this case, a business organization is supporting the customer's complaint.*

The Letter   Dear Name:

Occasionally the Retailers Association receives complaints from customers about business in this area. The enclosed letter concerns your business. We felt it was important to forward this complaint to you because we know you want to maintain good customer relations.

Please give this matter your personal attention. Misunderstandings can usually be corrected when both parties cooperate.

The Retailers Association is only an information source. We neither resolve conflicts between businesses and their customers nor do we make judgments about the situation. However, if a potential customer asks us if an unusual number of complaints have been lodged against a particular business, we do answer honestly.

Please advise us about this situation and how it was resolved.

Sincerely,

Toxic Waste Disposal

Situation   *This company has taken steps to dispose of toxic wastes properly. At the same time, the company has provided the option to employees.*

The Letter   Waste Disposal Company will be making a special pick-up of toxic wastes from XYZ premises Saturday morning. They have agreed to accept items from employees as well.

Bring your old batteries, paint cans, gasoline cans, kerosene heaters, and other items unsuitable for landfills to the west entrance between 9 a.m. and 12 noon.

Please help do your part to protect our environment. Bring your toxic wastes next Saturday so they can be disposed of properly.

Trade Show Follow-Up

Situation   *Businesspeople participate in industry trade shows to promote their services, introduce new products, network with other people in their industry, find new customers, and meet with current customers. When the show is over, salespeople make it a point to write to many of those they met at the show.*

The Letter   Dear Name:

Thanks for stopping by our booth at the Phoenix Trade Show last week. It was indeed pleasant to talk to someone from Connecticut. I used to live near Candlewood Lake, and I miss the woods and view, especially at this time of year.

Enclosed is a packet of information describing in more detail what XYZ Mobile Buildings can do for you. Our company provides:

- On-site delivery within one week

- Extensive inventory of sizes and styles

- Custom designs to match your specifications

- Options to rent, lease, or buy

- Units for multiple uses, such as sales trailers and elementary school classrooms.

I will be in the Seattle area soon and would welcome the opportunity to meet with you again. I'll give you a call in the next few days to set up a mutually convenient time.

Sincerely,

Ultimatum Letter Received in Error

Situation

Mistakes happen. When one occurs, you should document the error. It may also be necessary to send a copy of your letter to all parties concerned. By doing this, you are making sure that everyone has been notified.

The Letter

Dear Name:

I was very surprised to receive your letter dated March 24 stating that my account had been turned over to a collection agency. As the attached photocopy of my canceled check shows, the account was paid in full on January 27.

Please correct your records to show that this account was paid in full and on time. In addition, a notice to this effect should be sent to the collection agency and credit bureau to show that this account is not now—and was never—in arrears.

I look forward to seeing copies of your correspondence on this.

Sincerely,

Unsolicited Recommendation

Situation

It is worth the effort to write a letter praising someone's hard work. Send the letter to the person's supervisor or manager. Unsolicited recommendations are meaningful and appreciated by both the employer and employee.

The Letter

Dear Name:

I want to let you know what an excellent job John Doe has been doing for us. We are in the midst of the harvest season when every day counts.

John's prompt responses to our service calls have been outstanding. His knowledge and ability to make quick repairs on our harvest equipment have made it possible for us to minimize down time and ultimately maintain our original harvest schedule.

We appreciate John's work and great service and thought you should know.

Sincerely,

Upgrade Offer

Situation   *This letter is an offer to review a current system and make recommendations for upgrading.*

The Letter   Dear Name:

You have been using our accounting system for three years now, and perhaps it is time to review your company's current needs. It may well be time to update this system to take advantage of the latest software and recordkeeping abilities.

Our latest model cash registers are more tamperproof then ever and can be easily networked into your existing system. By updating your main system, you can also take advantage of our point-of-purchase system. This network system updates cash and inventory records every time a purchase is made.

Please take a moment to study the enclosed brochure. It has been our experience that the cost of the update will pay for itself within the first year. I will be in your area in a few weeks and will be in touch with you then. In the meantime, if you have any questions, give me a call.

Sincerely,

Verification of Employment

Situation   *This letter merely verifies information. Company policy prevents the writer from offering any information on the employee's performance. The current legal climate is such that many companies are now adopting this policy.*

The Letter   Dear Name:

Thank you for your inquiry of December 3.

Mr. John Doe was an employee of XYZ Corporation. He worked here from July 19, 1993 to November 4, 1997. His job titles were: shipping clerk, warehouse supervisor, assistant shipping manager, and most recently, shipping manager.

Sincerely,

Welcome New Employee

Situation

A friendly letter from a manager welcoming a new employee will help that person feel that accepting the position was the right choice.

The Letter

Dear Name:

Welcome aboard! I am quite pleased you accepted our offer of employment.

Your industry knowledge and management experience should serve you well in your new position with XYZ as Southwest Regional Manager.

I'll see you soon at our upcoming meeting in Houston. I look forward to hearing of your future successes.

Warm regards,

Welcome to New Resident

Situation   *Many businesses contact new homeowners in the area to introduce their goods and services. The following letter offers special discounts to entice potential customers.*

The Letter   Dear Name:

Welcome to the area! Now that the job of moving is over, we would like to tell you about ourselves. Smith's Drug Store is known and respected in this community for quality and service. Our registered pharmacists are happy to answer any questions. We work closely with the medical professionals in this area and pay close attention to your medical and related needs.

To introduce you to the many goods and services we offer, we are enclosing a discount certificate good toward any purchase in our store.

Please stop by to say hello. We look forward to serving you.

Sincerely,

Written Authorization Needed

Situation *This memo is a request for written authorization. The situation has already been resolved, so the writer does not need to review the decision-making process.*

The Letter Dear Name:

At the last department head meeting, it was decided to increase our inventory level to 10% more than last season. Doing this will exceed my purchasing authority by $25,000, so I need your official go-ahead.

Please indicate your approval on this letter, and I'll take care of it from there. A handwritten note from you will satisfy our finance people. Thanks.

Regards,

Wrong Item Shipped Twice

Situation   *Repeated shipping errors to the same customer clearly indicate a business situation that needs attention. But while the problem is being investigated, an unhappy customer needs some consideration as well.*

The Letter   Dear Name:

We regret very much that we have duplicated an incorrect shipment again. Please accept our sincere apologies. Corrective measures have been taken, and the merchandise you ordered should be on your doorstep the day after tomorrow.

Please return the incorrectly shipped items at our expense. A shipping label and airbill are enclosed for your convenience.

As a token of our appreciation for your cooperation, we are enclosing a gift certificate that can be applied toward your next order. Thank you for your patience.

Sincerely,

Index

About the Author

Ann Poe is a professional writer, author, and consultant. She is president of The Cade Group, Inc. and lives in Crystal Lake, Illinois.